Football in Richmond

Football in Richmond

1949 Richmond Rebel Champions

Pictured above are the dynamic defensive warriors who led the Rebels to the Atlantic Coast Football League Championship in the autumn of 1949. Pictured; first row (l-r): Mike Rubish, Bill Hornick, Paul Adams, Mike Phillips, John Leon, Grover Jones and Cotton Howell; second row (l-r): George Teufel, Al Drulls, Ben Raimondi, Byron Gillory

Front Cover:

Rare photograph of the 1949 Richmond Rebels Championship offensive team. Pictured; first row (l-r): Denver Mills, Al Helslander, Fritz Laurinatius, Joel Williams, Bob Mirth, Chester Fritz, Bob Nelson; second row (l-r): Lynn Chewning, Fred Cooper, Joe Corn, Paul Rickards

Back Cover:

Two of Richmond's finest footballers, NFL Hall of Famer Willie Lanier and All-Pro running back Ken Willard.

FOOTBALL IN RICHMOND

"Photographic Memories Of The Old Days"

Ron Pomfrey

Parker Field 1950
A "raccoon's coat" view from the stands at historic Parker Field on the Boulevard. This grand old stadium hosted many of the local high school's premier "Friday Nite" games. Also noted, this was the gridiron where the author viewed his first college football game, a Thanksgiving Day contest!

Copyright © 2011 by Ron Pomfrey
ISBN 978-0-615-52919-6

Published by W. Ronald Pomfrey, Sr. Mechanicsville, Virginia

Library of Congress CIP applied for.

For all general information contact W. Ronald Pomfrey, Sr. at:
Telephone 804-730-7700, Fax 804-427-5300, Email w.pomfrey@comcast.net
For customer service and orders: Telephone 804-730-7700

All rights reserved. No part of this book may be reproduced or transmitted in any form whatsoever without prior written permission from the publisher.

This book is dedicated to the memory of my sisters, Sharon Marie Pomfrey and Carolyn Pomfrey Walsh, who left us much too soon.

CONTENTS

PRE-GAME WARMUP
Acknowledgements 6
Introduction 7

FIRST QUARTER
Richmond Arrow 1922-1942 8
Exhibitions-The NFL Comes to Town 16
Richmond Rebels I 1946-1950 30

SECOND QUARTER
Richmond Rebels II 1964-1966 38
The Tobacco Bowl 46
Richmond Mustangs 1967 54

HALFTIME
Memorabilia & Artifacts 62

THIRD QUARTER
Richmond Roadrunners 1968-1969 80
The Collegiate Game 88
Richmond Saints 1970 102

FOURTH QUARTER
Richmond Football Field of Legends 108
High School Classics 128

OVERTIME
The Way We Were 142
To The Showers: About the Author 143

ACKNOWLEDGEMENTS

As in the game of football, when the final whistle blows, the Head Coach is only successful if he surrounded himself with a knowledgeable group of assistant coaches. Special thanks are in order to the following assistants that went above and beyond in the giving of their time, insight, encouragement, memories, and support: Lou Anderson, George Borden, Gary Denton, Walter Donovan, Charles Drinkard, Buddy Gregory, Griss Howard, Susan Johnson, Ron Martin, Al Mills, Jimmy Patterson, Rick Phelps, Caroline Smyth, Lloyd Swelnis, Sommer Wickham, Bob Weirup and Pat Winston.

Special thanks also to Debby Ring-Ashworth for her timeless assistance, her meticulous reviews, and her editing expertise.

Very special thanks to my wife, Sandy, for her continuing support and who allows a man with a boy's love for football to not get in the way of a happy marriage.

UNIVERSITY OF RICHMOND SPIDERS CHAMPIONSHIP TEAM
Even though this book portrays "Photographic Memories of the Old Days," we'd be remiss not to honor and acknowledge the accomplishments of our 2008 University of Richmond Football Spiders, National Champions! Congratulations, you lit the city's lamps!!

INTRODUCTION

As a purveyor and collector of Richmond football memorabilia and artifacts over the past forty years, I have developed a profound understanding and appreciation of the contributions made by our past gridiron greats. I have pursued every scrap of information and material that I could possibly acquire with the passion of a youngster suiting up for his first football game. With the addition of each new relic to my collection, my knowledge of the history of the game of football in Richmond grew. From our first collegiate clash in 1881, our Arrow wonder teams of the 1920s & 1930s, the raucous Rebels of the 1940s, our marvelous Mustangs of the 1960s or the woeful Saints of 1970, the memories of our Richmond football players and teams are forever etched in the history of our fair city. These events in Richmond's football past rekindled many fond football memories of my youth; my first official pigskin a "Doak Walker" model, my first real football game at Hotchkiss Field, attempting to attach a "one bar" face mask to my helmet, my "Choo-Choo" Justice shoulder pads which were secured by my #3 Ralph Guglielmi football jersey and "blood & guts" in the backyard. And do you remember when...

We "hiked" the football.
The goalpost were wood and at the goal line.
We had white "nite time" footballs.
The drop-kick was used.
Plays were drawn up in the huddle.
We used wrap-around hip pads.
We drank from the ladle in a metal water bucket.
Our pass plays were a button hook or go long.
We had two-way players.
Once you tackled a player, you had to hold him down.
Salt tablets were in vogue.
High-tops were the football shoes of the day.
Parker Field was used for football.
"Statue of Liberty" was our surprise play.
"Little Johnny" was at our Tobacco Bowls.
And our homecoming queens were only female.

To me these many fond memories of my early football days are priceless and I will cherish them forever. It is my hope that while reading this book and viewing the photography you will share with me the pleasure I have had in presenting Football in Richmond.

RICHMOND ARROW UNDEFEATED TEAM 1931

A resplendent image of this football powerhouse captures our Richmond Arrow footballers at the base of the hill of old City Stadium. A juggernaut of a team in the 1930s, it was not uncommon for crowds of 12,000 to turn out and cheer on the Arrow squad. The team won the state semi-pro championship in 1932. Outfitted to the "nines" in football uniforms of the period, this is one of the earliest known Arrow team photos. Simply the fact that it exists is a beautiful thing.

FIRST QUARTER
RICHMOND ARROW 1922-1942

The Arrow Athletic Club, Genesis 1922
Emblematic of something straight, and oh so true
George Blume got it started, Frank Rowlett suggested the name
Who could have imagined then, The Richmond Arrow would gain so much fame
Laying out the first gridiron, with pick and shovel they did wield
Built it on the site, today we call Hotchkiss Field
No uniforms or equipment, little football in these times
But members soon secured some, by soliciting nickels and dimes
Polars, Bear Cats, Ginter Park & the Blues, these teams would get no pity
The Arrow Team was often undefeated, and Champions of our City
Into the 30s, Richmond Arrow, a powerhouse in our region
Join the Dixie League, to the stadium fans flock like a legion
There was a player walkout in the season of '36
Manager Meanley brought in new ones, this revolt he did nix
The Arrows finished on top, these gridders they did beam
Guard Pratali, Quarterback Fenlon, named to All-League team
Year of '37 Redskins and Sammy Baugh, at stadium for all to see
Skins whip our Arrows, Lyle Graham Dixie League MVP
Finishing in second place, for the season of '38
Irvin Payne, Allen Keen our All-Stars, on a team not so great
1939, Arrows win regular season race
Portsmouth steals our championship, brings in a ringer "ACE"
A third place finish, 1940 was the year
Conner wins league MVP, as a runner had no peer
Season of '41, fourth place finished seemed so bleak
Could not see the future, not even a short brief peek
The war would come, Dixie League shuts down year of '42
There's no football team in Richmond, no opponents for us to boo
Arrow players of the past, had played their final game
But their memories I'll always cherish, In the Arrows' Hall of Fame.

Lyle Graham

This mountain of a man, standing 6'3" tall and weighing 210 pounds first appeared in the Arrow uniform in 1936, after a stellar college career as a center for legendary football coach Glenn Thistlethwaite at the University of Richmond. Hovering over the pigskin as the Arrows center, Graham quickly distinguished himself as one of the league's premier players. In the season of 1937, big number 34 was named the Dixie League's MVP.

Leroy Ford

Richmond fans will remember this gifted guard out of Thomas Jefferson High School, who plied his trade at Randolph-Macon College before becoming an intricate part of the Arrow line. Known for his uncanny skill of placing the oppositions' defenders on their backside, Ford opened gaping holes for the stable of Arrow running backs during the early 1940s. If playing today, his blocking expertise would make him worthy of All-Madden status.

Sam Lankford

Sam distinguished himself with the Arrows as a 178-pound kicker, running back and end in the late 1920s and early 1930s. He played his college ball at William & Mary, also on the gridiron of Hampton and the Apprentice School. The highlight of his career with the Arrows came in 1932, when he was voted Richmond's Outstanding Player of the Year.

Howard Haithcock

This 188-pound end was one of the original Richmond Arrows from the inaugural season of 1922. Number 23 on the scorecard, Haithcock played in the trenches, alternating between end and tackle. In the season of 1933 he was named the Arrows MVP, while manhandling many opposing lineman. Howard also played two years of football at Fork Union Military Academy.

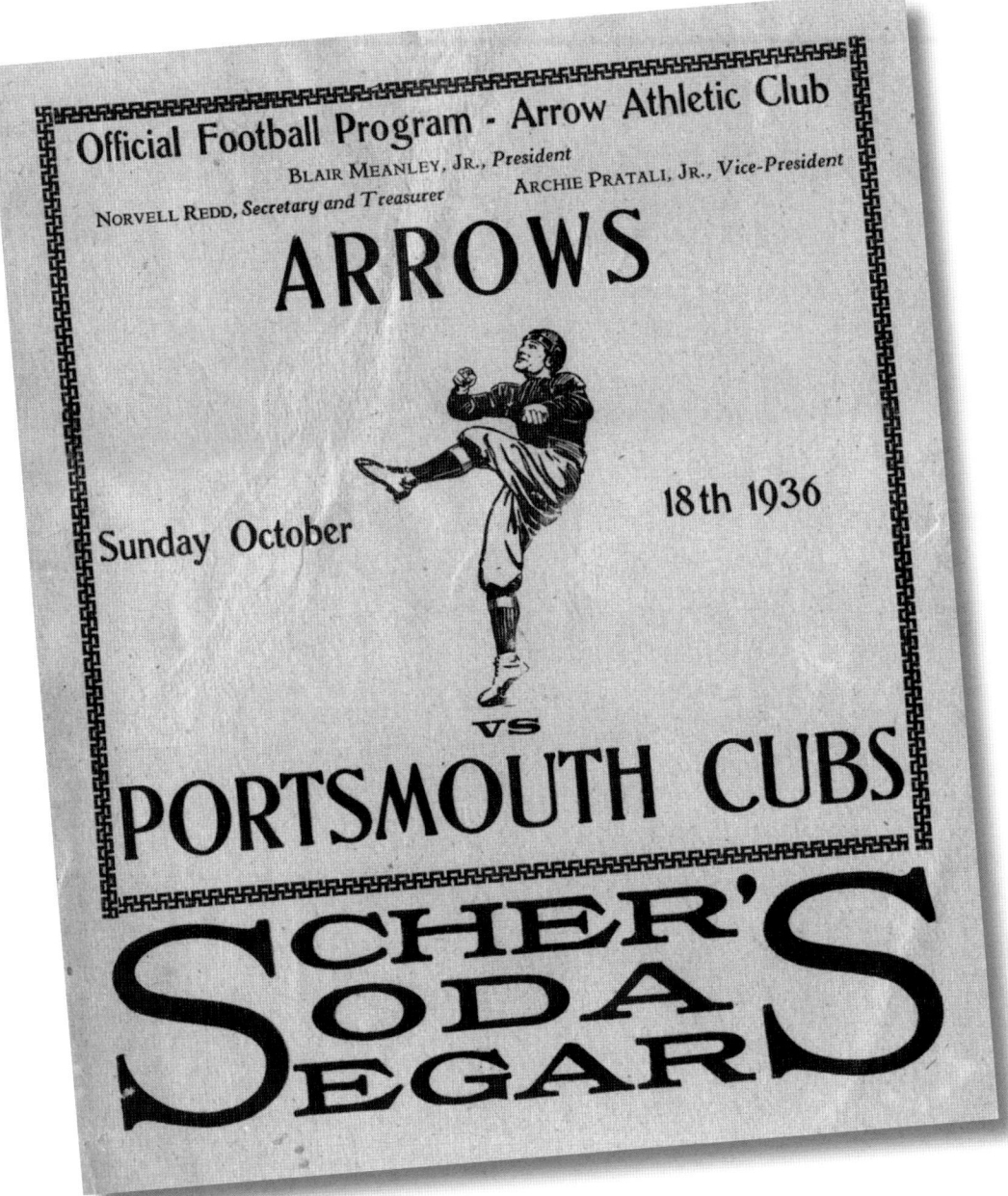

Richmond Arrow's Football Program 1936
A surviving example of extreme rarity seen here is a vintage football program of our Richmond Arrows. This Richmond football relic boast player rosters, Arrow Athletic Club hierarchy, game officials, starting line-ups and fascinating period ads. The game was played on Sunday, October 18th and pitted our Arrows against the Portsmouth Cubs.

Mush De Lotto

This powerful 187 pound running back played his college ball at Randolph-Macon College where his coach, Norman Sheppard, described him as "the greatest back, guard or tackle that ever played for him". Plying his trade as a runner for the Arrows, his star shined the brightest in 1939 when he led the team to the Dixie League regular season title and being named to the All-League Team. In 1934 Mush was named the Richmond Arrows MVP; he also spent time as an assistant football coach at Randolph-Macon College.

A. B. Conner

Conner starred for the Arrows as a shifty running back and quarterback in the late 1930s and early 1940s. A three year letterman at the University of Virginia, Conner's transition to the pro game came with ease. This premier running back was named the Dixie League's MVP in 1940 while rushing for 435 yards, catching 8 passes for 149 yards and completing 20 passes for 176 yards.

Vic Kreiter

This resourceful, skillful and keen minded 210 pound tackle promoted many of opposition to the "second string" with his bone jarring hits. Kreiter, a Chase City native, played his college ball at Emory & Henry College prior to displaying his talents for the Arrows during the seasons of 1940 and 1941. After his stint with the Arrows, this gallant gentleman served as principal of Highland Springs High School.

Irvin Payne

Irvin epitomized the "Cadillac" of guards for the Dixie League during the late 1930s. He cemented his place in the annals of the great Arrow players by being named as All-League Guard for 3 consecutive seasons, 1937-38-39. "Mr. Consistency" brought a flaming spirit to the club and was named their head coach for the season of 1940. Irvin played his college football on the gridiron of Emory & Henry College where he was captain of the team in 1936.

Perry Schultz

This three year letterman out of the University of Richmond distinguished himself with the Arrows in the seasons of 1935-1936. As a 165 pounder he was remarkably fast, had a knack for finding the ball carrier and delivering punishing tackles from his safety position.

Tom "Potsy" Jones

A former NFL star guard took the reins as head coach of the Arrows for the season of 1939. During his tenure in the NFL from 1930-1938 he played for four different teams including the Green Bay Packers and the New York Giants. His Arrow team instilled a healthy dose of fear in their opponents and finished the Dixie League regular season on top with a 6-1 record.

EXHIBITIONS - THE NFL COMES TO TOWN

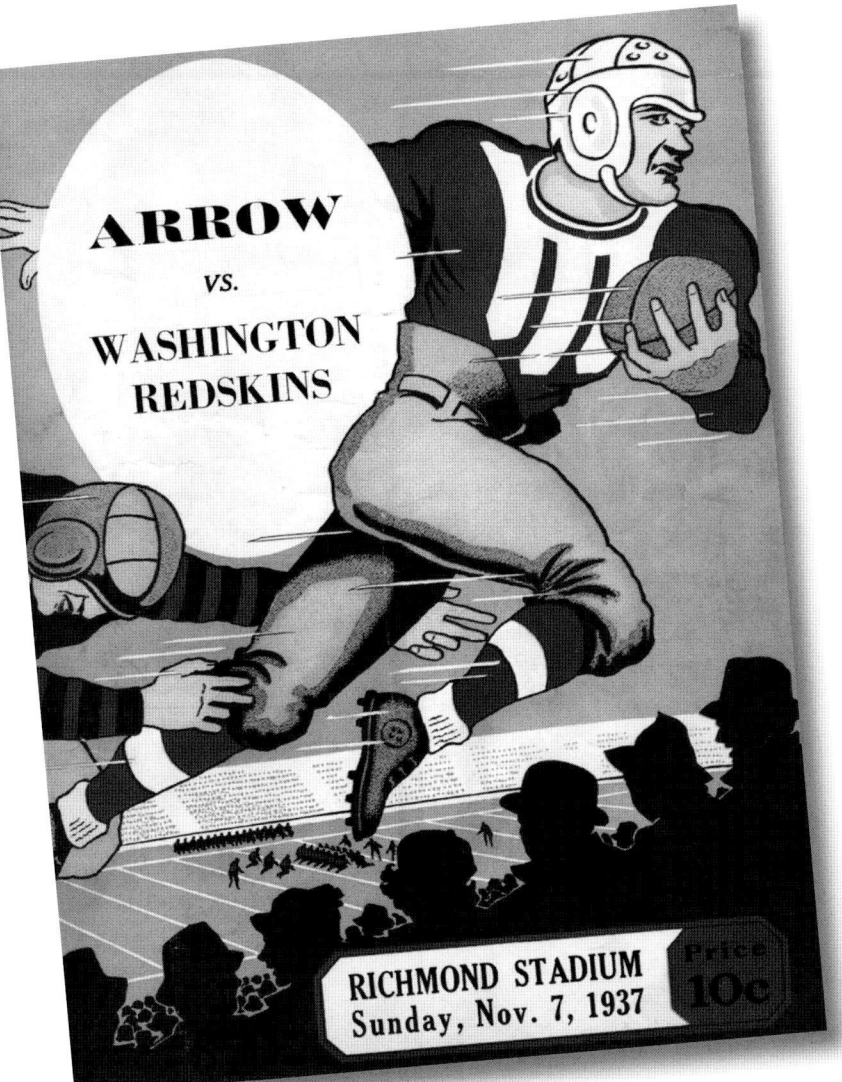

WASHINGTON REDSKINS VS ARROW, NOVEMBER 7, 1937

This old school football relic harkens back to an era when the game was played without the promise of a six or seven figure salary. George Preston Marshall, the Redskin's owner, brought his band of players to Richmond's City Stadium to play our Richmond Arrow team on this brisk November afternoon. Led by Riley Smith, Cliff Battles, Turk Edwards and Slingin' Sammy Baugh, the Redskins *skunked* the Arrows by a score of 30-0. As reported in the Richmond Times-Dispatch, "after the game Baugh was mobbed by hundreds of autograph-seekers, Sammy graciously consented to sign and was still going strong in the center of the mob after the grand stands were deserted." The Redskins went on to the height of football superiority by winning the NFL Championship in the season of 1937.

FIRST QUARTER
THE NFL COMES TO TOWN

Some called them exhibitions, when major league footballers came to town
The fans would pack City Stadium, they came from all around
George P. Marshall brought his Redskins, NFL Champs in '37
The opposition our Richmond Arrows, a fine football eleven
Many stars on the gridiron, but Sammy Baugh was the hero
That football juggernaut from Washington beat our Arrows, the score 30-0.
Skins return in '38, to play our Arrow team
Could the Richmonders upset the World Champions, last year's loss be redeemed
Touchdowns there were many, to the end zone they did flock
Finding pay dirt was Millner, Carroll, Baugh, and the talented Frank Filchock
A victory for our gridders, today not in the mix
Our Arrows fell to Washington, score 51-6.
New Year's Day 1941, or so the legend's told
Richmond All-Stars vs Norfolk All-Stars, first annual Smoke Bowl
Home team featured Marshall Goldberg All-American, and Jim Gillette from UVA
Norfolk had drop kicker Pete Sachon; "Daddy Long Legs" McFadden, making hay
When the final gun was sounded, the points there were few
All-Stars from Norfolk had 16, our Richmonders only 2.
September 8, 1946 Jock Sutherland brings his Pittsburgh Steelers to our city
To engage our Dixie League Rebels, fans were so giddy
Art Jones and "Bullet" Bill Dudley, oh how they ran the ball
Two Steeler high stepping runners, our Rebels could not stall
Final score 55-6, when all was said and done
But 11,000 fans showed up to cheer, under a hot September sun.
George Halas and his Chicago Bears arrive, fall of 1950
Luckman, Lujack and Blanda, these NFL stars, quite nifty
Our Richmond Rebels AFL Champs, hoping not to be the Bear's meal
If our guys in Red & White can keep it close, an upset we could steal
Three quarters done, one score down, one quarter left to play
Could our Richmond gridders pull it off, on this historic day
Two touchdowns in last two minutes, the Bears did win the game
Too many Hall of Famers on that team, for our Rebel squad to tame.

EXHIBITIONS - THE NFL COMES TO TOWN

GEORGE PRESTON MARSHALL

This graduate of Randolph-Macon College in Ashland was awarded an NFL franchise for Boston in 1932. In 1937 he moved his team to Washington and the rest is history. Known for exploits and innovations as an owner, he was the first to introduce gala halftime shows, a marching band, a fight song and embrace the new medium of television in the 1950s. As owner of the Washington Redskins, he had the reputation as a "hands-on" leader who built one of the NFL's real powerhouses on the football field. During the period 1936 through 1945, the Redskins won six divisional and two NFL championships.

CLIFF BATTLES

On the Redskins November 7, 1937 visit to City Stadium, this "brainy" halfback (Phi Beta Kappa Scholar) almost single handedly beat our Richmond Arrows. Described in the football program as a "combination of wonder athlete, gentleman, scholar and fellow of friendship," Battles not only ran over our Arrows, but was the NFL's leading ground gainer for the 1937 season. He was the very first player to gain over 200 yards rushing in a single game. This Hall of Famer quit the game at the end of 1937 when the Washington owner refused to raise his salary above $4,000.

WAYNE MILLNER

Millner spells competitor in every sense of the word. This glue-fingered end, a two-time All-American choice out of Notre Dame, played a significant role as a receiver for the Redskins on their visits here in 1937 and 1938. Known to make the "clutch" play in crucial games, Wayne caught 55 yard and 77 yard passes for touchdowns in the 1937 championship victory over the Chicago Bears. After an illustrious six year career with the Redskins, Millner served his country for three years in the Navy and returned to the Redskins as a player-coach in 1945.

ALBERT "TURK" EDWARDS

This two-time All-American tackle out of Washington State University, starred for the Redskins in their 1937 contest against the Arrows. Known as a "60 Minute Man," Turk stood 6'2", weighed 260 pounds, and was a steam rolling blocker and smothering tackler. An acclaimed gridiron maintenance man, Turk had a 9 year career with the Boston/Washington Redskins, four years as an All-Pro Performer. In 1969 he was enshrined in the Pro Football Hall of Fame.

―――― Exhibitions - The NFL Comes To Town ――――

ARROW VS WASHINGTON REDSKINS, NOVEMBER 20, 1938

This vintage football program from the season of 1938 begged to be preserved. The Redskins brought their team of distinction, the 1937 NFL Champions, to grace the gridiron of Old City Stadium on this brilliant fall November afternoon. With a bagful of tricks and a star studded backfield, the Washington Redskins gave the Richmond local fans a glimpse of real showmanship in snowing under the Arrows 51-6. The Redskins were led by Frank Filchock, Wee Willie Wilkins, and Slingin' Sammy Baugh, who displayed his gridiron aerial artistry as the Time-Dispatch headlines rang out "Redskins Crush Richmond-Baugh Thrills with Long Passes."

"SLINGIN" SAMMY BAUGH

The raccoon coats came to City Stadium in droves to witness the legendary skills of this Redskin star in the fall of 1937 and 1938. A versatile player who combined extraordinary athleticism with quick thinking, it was said of Baugh, "where other quarterbacks could hit a dime at fifty paces, Sammy at the same distance can trim the hair of the lady on the dime." Baugh led the Redskins to victory over the Arrows in both exhibitions played here in the 1930s. This two-time All-American out of Texas Christian University had an illustrious 16 year NFL career with the Washington Redskins. Multi-talented, he often played quarterback, defensive back, and did the punting, and is the only NFL player to lead the league in passing, punting and interceptions in the same season. Slingin' Sammy was inducted into the Pro Football Hall of Fame in the charter class of 1963.

Exhibitions - The NFL Comes To Town

Richmond Arrow vs Pittsburgh Pirates, November 12, 1939

Dan Rooney, owner of the Pittsburgh Pirates, the National Football League "cellar dwellers," brought his winless squad of footballers to Richmond to square off against the Dixie League's undefeated Richmond Arrows. The Pirates, led by their charismatic coach Walt "Babe" Kiesling, went on to maul the Arrows 33-0, which was convincing evidence to local footballites, "that a wide gulf separates minor and major league professional football." The Pirates defeated only one NFL team in the season of 1939 and changed their name to "Steelers" before the 1940 season, with hopes and expectations of bringing the team luck.

Walt "Babe" Kiesling

This rugged, two-way lineman enjoyed a 34-year career as a player and coach in the National Football League. A NFL Hall of Famer, he was named to the All-Decade Team of the 1920s and also starred on the Chicago Bears' unbeaten juggernaut in 1934. As a coach, "Babe" led the Pittsburgh Steelers to a winning season in 1942. An apostle of smash mouth football and old school techniques, he often clashed with his talented athletes. One of the biggest blunders in Steeler history is attributed to Kiesling. When, as a head coach, he benched a young Pittsburgh born-and-bred Johnny Unitas through an entire training camp before cutting him, allowing the Baltimore Colts to acquire his rights. The rest is history!

ELBIE "ELBOWS" NICKEL

The headlines in the Richmond Times-Dispatch said it all, "Nickel Tallies Winning Marker," as the Steelers rally late in the fourth quarter to down our Richmond Rebels. "Elbows" hauled in a 57 yard touchdown pass and raced to pay dirt to seal the Steelers come from behind victory. Nickel had a twenty year career with Pittsburgh and is considered the best tight end in Steeler's history. A three sport star out of the University of Cincinnati, he was drafted by the Steelers in 1947. He served as Steeler captain, was voted their MVP, and made three Pro Bowl teams. A sure-handed tight-end, Nickel could block with the best of them and he caught the tough passes over the middle.

RICHMOND REBELS VS PITTSBURGH STEELERS, SEPTEMBER 7, 1949

Loaded with nostalgia, this vintage football program is for a game in which the NFL's Steelers had to rally from behind in the fourth quarter to defeat our Rebels 28-16. As the fourth quarter approached, the adoring public yearned for an upset, as our gallant line, led by Chester Fritz, Bob Mirth, Denver Mills and Cotton Howell, "AMBUSHED" the Steelers. In the end the NFLers established themselves as victors, led by the all-around play of Bill Walsh and Elbie Nickel. This valiant effort by our Rebels commanded the attention of footballers far and wide and the Rebels brought home the AFL Championship for Richmonders in this season of 1949.

Exhibitions - The NFL Comes To Town

Bill Dudley

Affectionately known as the "Bluefield Comet," "Bullet Bill," and "Bounding Bill," this legendary footballer from Bluefield, Virginia was one of the most dominate players to ever grace the gridiron in the state of Virginia. Leading the Steelers to a 55-6 victory over our Rebels, "Bounding Bill is the boy in the Steeler's offense, he's the workhorse, as well as the fancy stepper," as reported by a Times-Dispatch sports writer. In this contest Bill was the offensive star, running for 106 yards and passing for 57. As a collegian at the University of Virginia, Bill was a halfback, running, passing and kicking from that position. He was voted to All-American, All-Southern, All-State, and All-Conference teams in 1941 and 1942. As a NFL rookie in 1942, Bill led the league in rushing yards for the season and was named All-Pro. He also starred for the Detroit Lions and Washington Redskins. His legendary football career has led to him being the only individual ever awarded the Most Valuable Player awards in college, military service and professional levels. He is a member of the College Hall of Fame, Pro Football Hall of Fame and Virginia Sports Hall of Fame. The Downtown Club of Richmond, Virginia has sponsored The Bill Dudley Award, awarded each year to the state's top college football player.

Pittsburgh Steelers vs Richmond Rebels, September 8, 1946

This is a very special and rare remnant from a September football spectacle at old City Stadium. This contest pitted the NFL's Pittsburgh Steelers, led by their famous coach Jock Sutherland, against our Richmond Rebels. The game was played before a crowd of 11,000 spectators under a broiling afternoon sun, which took its toll on both the players and grandstanders. The Steelers "smashed" our Rebels 55-6, parading up and down the field to score eight touchdowns and rolling up 16 first downs to the Rebels none. The Steelers offense was led by former University of Virginia standout Bill Dudley and former University of Richmond star running back Art Jones.

Art Jones

This triple threat running back out of the University of Richmond by way of Suffolk, Virginia, came back to his old stomping grounds of City Stadium on this hot, sultry September afternoon. At 6'2" and 200 pounds, he was an exceedingly fast and shifty runner with a nose for the goal line. With the Richmond Spiders, Art excelled as a kicker, runner and passer that gained the respect and admiration of his opponents while being named to the All-Stars and All-Conference football teams. Art had many of his followers show up at City Stadium to watch their hometown star. This contingent was quite dismayed when Coach Sutherland chose to use Art very sparingly in the contest, saving him for "more important" league games.

Exhibitions - The NFL Comes To Town

George Halas - Sid Luckman

Shown here kneeling with his Hall of Fame quarterback, Sid Luckman, is George "Papa Bear" Halas, as they both review some of the plays he would be using against our Rebels. Halas was known for his inspiring halftime pep talks, and won eight NFL Championships throughout his illustrious career. The boys from Richmond must have given him somewhat of a scare for as the Times-Dispatch reported, "Coach Halas shed his double-breasted business suit at the half, and returned in working clothes of a sport shirt, gray flannels and baseball cap." Luckman, a five-time All-Pro NFL quarterback, used his rifle arm to toss three touchdown passes for the Bears' high-powered offense.

Richmond Rebels vs Chicago Bears, October 22, 1950

This ticket stub was in the shirt pocket of a fan on hand to see George Halas' "Monsters of the Midway" play our AFL Champion Richmond Rebels. The contest marked the first appearance of the famous Chicago Bear gridders in a game south of the Potomac River. Seventeen-thousand football enthusiasts were on hand to witness the game and retell the events of the day to their children and grandchildren years later. Our Rebels made a game of it, with the score 21-14 at the end of the third quarter; but then came the big offensive flurry of the "Windy City" squad and it reared back with all the fury of a Gulf hurricane - final score 47-14. Halas' heroes were led by veteran quarterback Sid Luckman, Notre Dame All-American Johnny Lujack, and little known defensive back George Blanda.

CHICAGO BEARS VS WASHINGTON REDSKINS, AUGUST 15, 1964

Hold this vintage program and you can almost smell the hot dogs at old City Stadium! "Papa Bear" Halas brought the World Champion Bears to Richmond to play mayhem with Bill McPeak's Redskins. A record crowd of 23,611 of Richmond's football fraternity turned out to view this "buffet of gridiron stardom," which included Mike Ditka, Sam Huff, Bobby Mitchell, Vince Promuto, Pat Richter, Doug Atkins, Richie Petitbon and Bill Wade. Redskin's quarterback Sonny Jurgensen was injured and did not play. On this humid August evening the teams' defenses held the offenses impotent, and Halas' Bears squeaked out a 14-13 victory. The most excitement of the evening was generated by a few fisticuff flurries. Skin's Vince Promuto squared off with Bear's Joe Lewis in the first half and Washington's Riley Mattson and Chicago's Steve Barnett exchanged a few blows after halftime.

SAM HUFF

The Washington Redskins traded the New York Giants for this dominant, All-Pro middle linebacker, hoping he would work his magic for the Skins in the season of 1964. In the pre-game introductions, Huff garnered the greatest ovation from our Richmond fans and maintained his reign of dominance from his middle linebacker position. Halas' "Big Back" offense only gained a little over 100 yards as Sam and his defensive unit employed a plausible strategy to limit the Bears' ground game. Known as one of the NFL's fiercest interference busters, Sam's legendary career included five Pro Bowl selections. He was named to the NFL 1950s All-Decade Team, Redskin's Ring of Fame, College Football Hall of Fame, and Pro Football Hall of Fame.

Exhibitions - The NFL Comes To Town

Smoke Bowl, January 1, 1941

Finding one of these vintage relics is like finding a trunk in your grandparent's attic; probably one of the few specimens still left on earth. This seventy year old football program was for the first ever Smoke Bowl, which featured the Richmond All-Stars against the Norfolk All-Stars, to benefit the Fireman's Mutual Aid Association. The teams featured many of the recently graduated collegiate football icons of their day. The Richmond All-Stars were truly a team of distinction with the likes of two-time All-American out of Pittsburgh Marshall Goldberg, former University of Virginia captain Jim Gillette, star tackle Frank Albert of Notre Dame, and University of Richmond star center Ed Merrick. The Norfolk All-Stars were coached by former North Carolina great George Stirnweiss and their gridders who commanded national attention included Clemson's "Daddy Long Legs" Banks McFadden, guard Woody Gray of VMI, and "Pistol Pete" Sachon of Catholic University. This assemblage of acclaimed gridiron greats battled tooth-n-nail throughout the afternoon and culminated with a 16-2 victory for the All-Stars from Tidewater. The All-Stars from each team performed to the delight of the 7,000 local fans. This New Year's Day Blue Ribbon Event's pageantry was as fascinating and endearing as the game itself.

Jim Gillette

Jim's exploits on the gridiron were legendary. From his days on the turf in Courtland, Virginia, to captain of the University of Virginia eleven, to his spectacular touchdown catch in the 1945 NFL Championship game, Jim was known to garner fame wherever he played, including his six seasons in the NFL. Even though the Richmond All-Stars possessed a stable of outstanding running backs, he still averaged 15 yards per carry in this All-Star tilt, and had a superlative defensive game. An exemplar of clean football, Jim was known throughout the football circles as a true "Virginia Gentleman."

Marshall "Biggie" Goldberg

A two-time All-American out of the University of Pittsburgh, "Biggie" led the Panthers to back-to-back National Championships in 1936 and 1937. This all-purpose back was the Smoke Bowl's leading ground gainer as he "zigged and zagged" the gridiron at City Stadium on this storied day. Whether returning punts and kickoffs, or from the line of scrimmage, once "Biggie" had the pigskin he performed to the delight and fascination of our local fans. This spectacular performance vaulted him to his eight season professional career with the Chicago Cardinals, where he helped lead them to the NFL Championship in 1947.

Richmond Rebels I - 1946-1950

1949 Richmond Rebels - AFL Champions

There was something historic happening on the grassy field we called City Stadium in the fall of 1949. The gridiron aggregation of Rebel football players posted a glittering record, with eight regular season victories and 2 playoff wins as the Rebels became the American Football League champs. Displaying obvious superiority, Richmond placed five players on the All-League Team including end Denver Mills, guard Bob Mirth, center Boyd Williams, halfback Fred Cooper, and fullback Byron Gillory.

FIRST QUARTER
RICHMOND REBELS I 1946-1950

Four years without a football team, war had left quite a mix
Richmond Arrow renamed Rebels, for the season of '46
First game with Pittsburgh Steelers, Jock Sutherland's men in town
11,000 fans pack the stands, but end-zone was seldom found
Four players named to All-League team, Quarterback Knox was our key
Led the league in passing, our Rebels ended seven and three.
1947, new owner Harry Seibold, season tickets he did sell
Started the year in Dixie League, by October the AFL
Many ups and downs on the gridiron, before their swan song was sung
With Coach McEver at the helm, Rebels ended the year 6-3-1.
Our glue-fingered end Denver Mills, catching passes our quarterback would loft
And Reynolds the league's scoring champ, leads our '48 Rebels to the playoffs.
A 6-4 record, many of our locals they did shine
There was Jack Wilbourne running the ball and Bobby Thalman anchoring the line
The season of '49, playing with vigor and true grit
Rebels win championship, led by "Cannonball" and Chester Fritz
Then there was Gillory and our own Lynn Chewning running the oblong ball
While Laurenaitis and Doc Savage paced the defense, opponents they would maul.
1950 fate arrives, the AFL has not a clue
League starts the year with six teams, ends with only two
Our Rebels are still winning, Erie Vets make it a race
Game snowed out in November, December 3rd playing for first place
Led by quarterback Rickards and safety Ellis' two touchdowns
The Rebels are victorious, as the final whistle sounds
No teams for '51, as the league soon realized its fears
But our Richmond Rebels were AFL champs, for two consecutive years!

RICHMOND REBELS I - 1946-1950

1946 RICHMOND REBELS

No stars, only "grunts of the gridiron" formed the nucleus for the first Richmond Rebels team. This contingent of footballers, led by their coach Mac McEver, was strong on fundamentals and meticulously performed their assignments, which led them to a 7-3 Dixie League record.
Top Row: (left to right) Stewart, Ellington, Gibson, Tharp, Parlow, Tiller, Ford, Coach McEver
Middle Row: Lafoon, Butcher, Kratochvil, Kapriva, Driscoll, Pulley, Williams
Bottom Row: Lucente, Trunzo, Gonda, Hill, Siegfried, Vetter

CLYDE "DUKE" ELLINGTON

A stalwart on defense for the Rebels in the season of 1946, this 210 pound guard-tackle was both mentally bright and physically tough as a leader of the Rebel lineman. #73's star shone brightly in this "re-established" Dixie League season. "Duke" had previously starred collegiately as a lineman for the VMI Keydets.

Ben Raimondi
Seen here sweeping the right end against the Paterson Panthers, Ben displayed spurts of brilliance carrying the pigskin in the season of 1948. Skilled as both a runner and quarterback, he nearly led the Rebels to an upset victory over the Chicago Bears in 1949. Collegiately, Ben played at Indiana, where he was known as a hard-nosed competitor both on and off the football field.

Courtney "Red" Driscoll
A little All-American for Marshall College and star on the gridiron at Benedictine High School, "Red" had a penchant for making the big play. A multi-talented performer for the Rebels in 1946, he was known as an aggressive leader on the field who gave this newly established team instant credibility. He helped lead the Rebels to a second place finish in the Dixie League with a record of 7 wins, 3 losses.

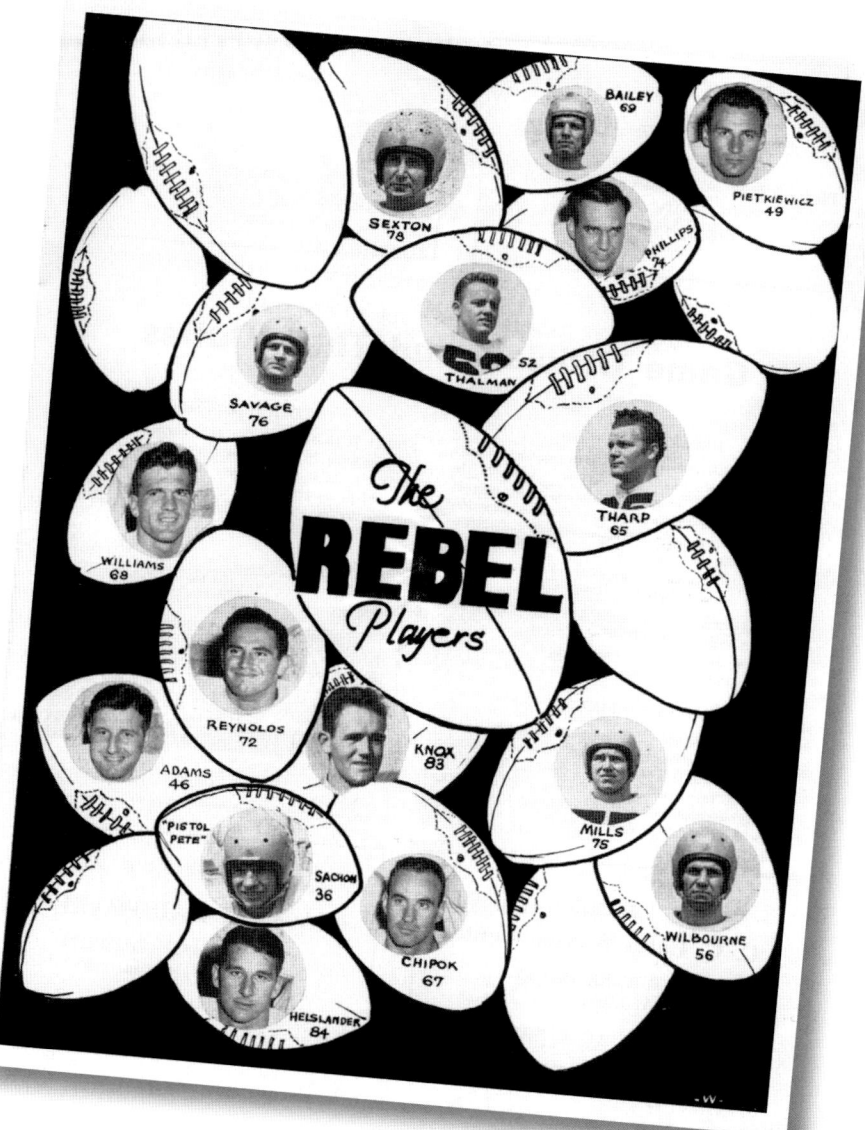

1948 RICHMOND REBELS

These facial images of our footballers from 1948 take us back to a time of true grit and charisma. Toughness meant playing without a facemask, hitting hard enough to knock the opponent senseless, and leaving a mammoth imprint on the opposing quarterback. This gang was led by halfback Jim Reynolds (Dixie League leader in scoring and interceptions), Pete Sachon (league leader in punting average), tackle "Big" Jim Tharp (6'5" 235 pounder out of Notre Dame), and quarterback-receiver duo of Glenn Knox and Denver Mills. The Rebels ended the season in second place of the Dixie League with a 6-4 record.

GLENN KNOX

As a rookie quarterback for the Rebels in 1946, Knox produced an astonishing set of numbers while leading the team to a second place finish with a 7-3 Dixie League record. Known for his big play tactics and leadership, Glenn was an All-League selection and the league's leading passer in the season of 1946. As a star end at William & Mary, he made pass-snagging look easy and showcased his speed in the open field. One of the finest ends ever developed in a Virginia college, he was both All-State and All-Conference for the Tribe in 1941 and 1942.

FRED "CANNONBALL" COOPER

Historically, the "first negro ever signed by a Southern professional football team," Cannonball quickly became the darling of Richmond football fans. This bona fide action shot shows the fire in his eyes and tenacity running through his veins as he rips free from a would-be tackler in his pursuit to pay dirt. Cannonball's legendary runs left spectators gasping in awe as he led the Rebels to the AFL championships in 1949 and 1950. Topping the league in scoring and ground gaining in 1949, this pile driving runner out of Virginia Union University electrified fans with his flair for the dramatic while assaulting the opponents goalline.

Chester "The Chief" Fritz

This gridiron giant (6'3", 230 pound) tackle, who was All-Conference and second team All-American at the University of Missouri, helped redefine Richmond's football reputation in the championship seasons of 1949-1950. Smitten by the game, Fritz spearheaded the offensive line of the Rebels, whose demeanor reflected their seriousness of purpose. On the playing field, Fritz was a ferocious competitor who demonstrated both poise and confidence, and is truly one of the Rebels all-time greats.

Keith "Moley" Molesworth

For the season of 1949, Harry Seibold, the owner of our Richmond Rebels, secured the services of Keith Molesworth as Head Coach. "Moley" had been the star quarterback of the Chicago Bears for 7 years during the 1930s, in a backfield that included Red Grange and Bronko Nagurski. With the "brainy" Molesworth at quarterback, the Bears won the NFL championship in 1932 and 1933. As head coach of our Rebels there was no "blood and thunder" in his pep talks, but his teams exemplified a mechanical perfection of a cohesive and well-disciplined squad. He quickly installed the Bears' version of the T-formation, which featured a fast, wide open style of play. An avalanche of touchdowns and victories followed and our Rebels were AFL champions under Molesworth in both 1949 and 1950. "Moley", a man of high character and a master of evaluating talent, was named Head Coach of the 1953 Baltimore Colts, in their first NFL season.

BILL KLIEN

From the halls of John Marshall High School to the gridiron of William & Mary, homegrown and accustomed to the friendly fans, Bill starred for the Rebels as both a fullback and end. Klien was like a charging buffalo, leaving opponents nursing their wounds and pride. A man of high character, he later was a leader of football officials in Richmond.

RICHMOND REBELS 1964

There was no surrender in this contingent of young footballers assembled by first year Head Coach Pete Pihos. Eager to prove they belonged in the Atlantic Coast Pro Football League, the Rebels won only 2 of their first seven games, but went undefeated in their final seven games, ending with a 8-5-1 record. Pictured: Front Row (l-r) Moran, Fisher, Smith, Irvin, Dickerson, Davenport, Rossi, B. Davis, J. Davis, Fields; Middle Row (l-r) Honea, Powell, Baker, McGinnis, Starnes, Sullivan, Christman, Zolak, Overcash, Joyner, Andrews, Kuhn, Coach Pihos; Back Row (l-r) Gwaltney, Rice, Raub, Aldrich, Blazevich, Kern, Denby, Aliffi, Evans, Craig, Fogle, Cooper, Coach Deter, Coach Wise

SECOND QUARTER
RICHMOND REBELS II 1964-1966

Oh such a void, thirteen years no pro football, what a pity
1964 Bob Spitler comes to town, forms the new Rebels for our city.
Vic Aliffi, first player signed, this linebacker oh so big
February Rebels granted franchise in Atlantic Coast Football League.
In need of a quarterback, to bring the fans through the gate
Rebs go out and sign Jim Rossi, the star from N. C. State.
Where do we find someone to Coach, this Rebels football team?
Spitler signs Pete Pihos, his resume just gleamed
Many players show up to be a Rebel, this team has set its mark
First practice in hot July, by the tennis courts at old Byrd Park
Joyner, Lamberti, Christman, a team Pihos must mold
August 1st, Newark Bears in town, Richmond's first Civitan Bowl
With Kuhn, Ames, Oscar and Davenport, this team was full of fun
Rebels undefeated in last seven games, final record 8-5-1.
1965, Appler, Alley, Irvin and Merv Holland, to provide a true bump
Happy Chandler, new commissioner, to the Continental League we did jump.
These gridiron gents quite exciting, as our fans came to see
Bill Barber led in pass snagging, Tony Koszarsky, team MVP.
No playoffs this fall season, championship would have to wait
Rebels ended 1965, winning 6 while losing 8
Season of '66, will new leadership get us over the hill
Markel recruits Steve Sucic to coach, hoping stadium seats he would fill.
With a few minor changes, would a championship not be far?
There's Joyner, Barber and Day, voted to the league's All-Stars
Could this be the year, many games Rebs would win?
Say it ain't so Joe, our pluses only 4, our minuses were 10.

Richmond Rebels II - 1964-1966

Rebels Coaching Staff 1965

This group of teaching perfectionists were led by head coach Pete Pihos, an All-American end at the University of Indiana and a five-time All-Pro selection with the Philadelphia Eagles. A dedicated staff of bright football minds were shooting for the championship in 1965, falling short of this goal, the Rebel team did bring drama of victory and defeat. Pictured (l-r): Pat Lamberti, Pete Pihos, Bruce Nunnally, Monte Williamson, Bob Harrison and Carl Wise

Jim Rossi

Versatility and dedication are the earmarks of this all-around quarterback out of North Carolina State. Quickly shifting to the free safety position for the Rebels, Jim dazzled the crowd with interception returns and his league leading punt returns in 1965. Jim also starred for our Mustangs in their storybook season of 1967, and in 1968 he was a player-coach for our Richmond Roadrunners.

RICHMOND REBELS DEFENSIVE TEAM 1965
Pictured here are the mainstays for the Rebels defense in the 1965 season. Even though there were only six victories in 1965, this spirited group of defenders of the goal line displayed an animalistic type of ability when attacking the opponents' offense. Pictured; Front-Four (l-r) Jim Townes, Luther Woodruff, Lewis Irvin, Gene Appler; Linebackers (l-r) Ken Honea, Don Christman, Gene Donaldson; Defensive Backs (l-r) Gary Arnold, Jim Rossi, Carl Kuhn, David Ames

BILL BARBER
Speed and deception were the qualities that made this wide receiver out of Florida A&M University a great pass catcher. A real crowd riser, when Bill got his hands on the ball his mission was to reach pay dirt. Truly a player of distinction, he also starred for the 1967 Mustangs and our Roadrunners in 1968.

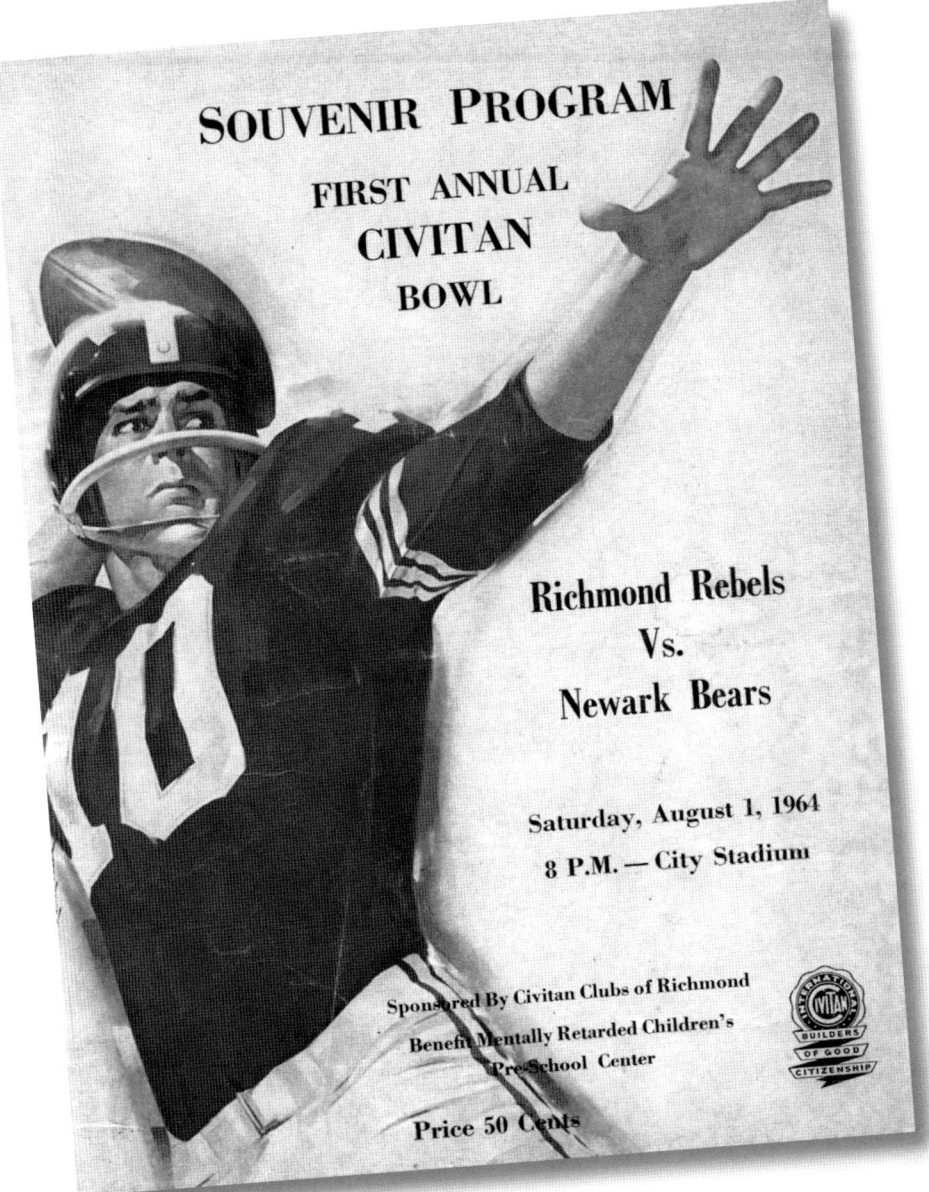

Civitan Bowl Program, August 1, 1964

The "Cork Popper" for our new Richmond Rebels came on August 1, 1964 against the Newark Bears. This was the First Annual Civitan Bowl and was played for the benefit of the Mentally Retarded Children's Pre-School Center, quite a noble cause for our Richmond Civitan Club to undertake. Displayed here is a scarce program from this landmark event in Richmond football. However, the lofty expectations of the fans at City Stadium soon evaporated as the wily veterans of the Newark Bears put a pasting on our football Rebels by a score of 39-7.

Don "Red" Christman

Truly a favorite of the "raccoon coats" in the stands, Red hails from the University of Richmond, where he was an All-Southern Conference performer and was drafted by the Boston Patriots. Known for his bone chilling tackles as the Rebels middle linebacker, Red's motto was "no system of play substitutes for knocking an opponent down." Red was also an integral part of our 1967 Mustangs and served as a player-coach for our 1968 Roadrunners.

Lewis Irvin

A burly 5'11", 240 pound defensive tackle out of Virginia State University, Irvin "handled ball carriers as though they were wooden soldiers." Known for his great strength and quickness, he had no match in his pursuit of ball carriers. In the 1965 season Lewis was runner-up in the team MVP voting and in 1966 was named to the Continental League All-Star Team.

TONY KOSZARSKY

There was jubilation in the stands when Tony toted the pigskin for our Rebels. This 5'8", 180 pound halfback out of North Carolina State was the heart of the offense during his three year tenure with the Rebels. Chosen as the team MVP in 1965, Tony was known as a squirming, twisting, dashing runner, who always performed his best in clutch games.

DUNNINGTON AND HUBBS IN ACTION, 1965

This massive but mobile offensive guard, #63 Fred Hubbs, appears to be telling running back Bob Dunnington, "just follow me" as the Rebel duo display some typical power football. At 6'2" and 240 pounds, Hubbs was known for his fierce blocking and mistake-free line play. Dunnington, a former Richmond Spider, possessed springy legs and could stop on a dime and veer the other way while finding his way to the end zone.

David Ames

Raw-boned, intense, hard-nosed are the best words to describe this defensive back out of the University of Richmond. This 5'11", 190 pounder played with a swagger as a star defender for the Rebels. When you lined up against #44 David Ames you got a taste of serious football. David also had a superlative season as a defensive back with our championship Mustangs in 1967. An ambassador for the game and true gentleman, David worked and resided in Richmond after his football career.

1965 Rebelettes

With their voices booming with spirit, this stable of young beauties brought many of the spectators to their feet, both cheering and trying to stay warm in the season of 1965. Their spirited enthusiasm and balanced perfection captured both the players' and fans' imagination. Pictured: Standing (l-r) Linda Ley, Carol Williams, Ginny McNeal, Dottie Abercrombie, Janice Livesay, Jane Armstrong, Pat Kelly, Sharon Smith, Pat Strang, Suzie Monahan, Mary Aliff; Knelling (l-r) Co-Captains Earle Elaine Bass and Dale Gatewood.

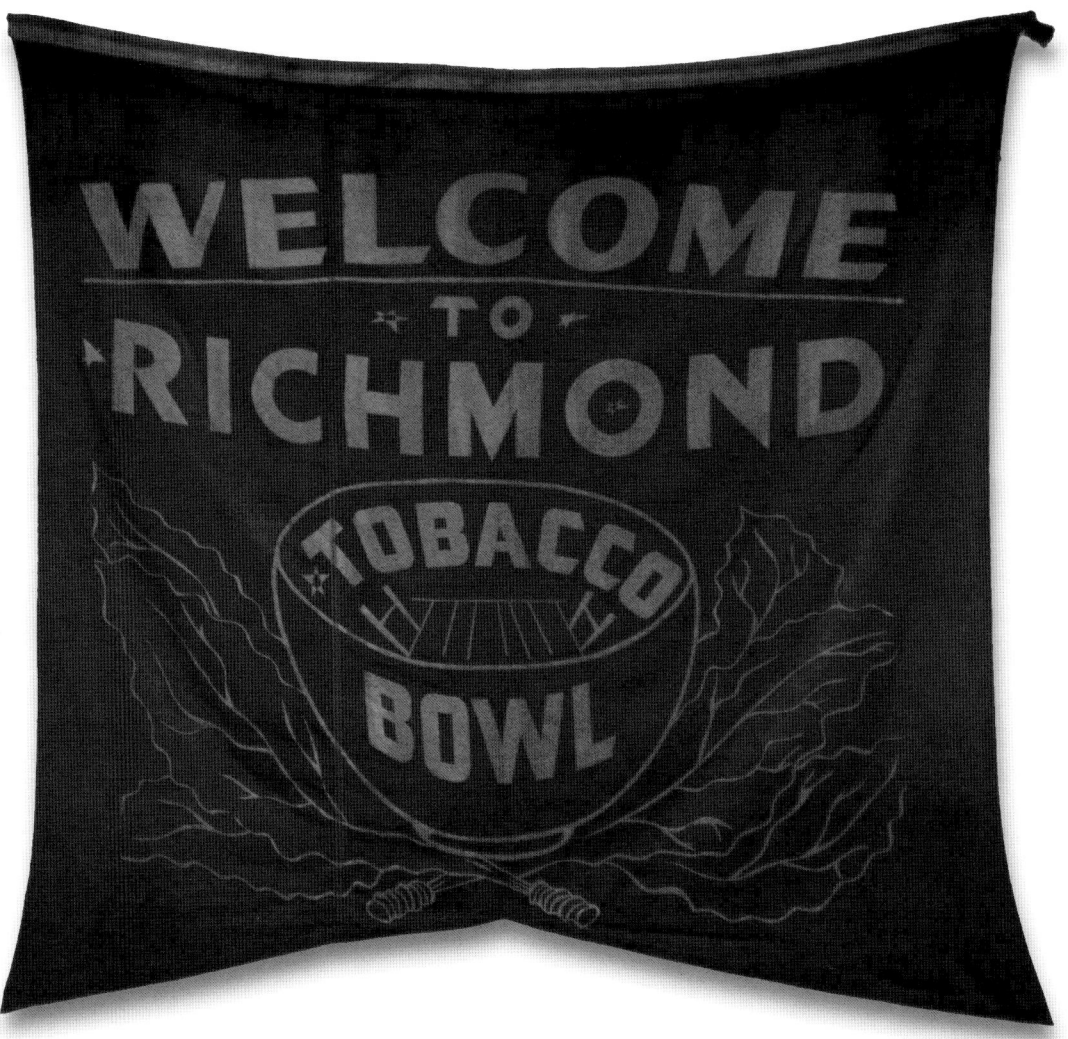

VINTAGE TOBACCO BOWL BANNER
Pictured above is an exceptional example of one of the rarest and most elaborately designed banners depicting Richmond's Tobacco Bowl. The banner measures 50" X 50" and the fancy design elements include a "Tobacco Bowl" encasing a football field nestled in tobacco leaves. Dating to the Tobacco Bowl's glory years of the early 1950s, the banners red and gold colors vividly express the spirit that this annual tilt encompassed.

SECOND QUARTER
THE TOBACCO BOWL

It started with Mr. Carlton, Chairman, the year was '49;
A festival, floats, football game and tobacco from a vine.
The Keydets from Lexington beat the Spiders, very first Tobacco Bowl game
With Frank Sinatra as the Marshall, Dorothy Kirsten was the dame.
Queens there were many, their beauty we did rate
Betty Barnette, Miss Hanover, was crowned in '58.
Celebrities they came; Edie Adams, Matt Dillion, Peter Graves to name a few;
But "Little" Johnny was the favorite; Raymond Burr in '62.
Such pageantry, illuminated parade; this event has become quite tall
We now have the Arena hosting the Grand Opening Ball.
All this pomp and circumstance, festivities it did yield
But all the footballers wanted to view the teams on the field.
With Virginia winning in 1950 and William & Mary in '51
Cavaliers again in '52, '53 the Spiders had some fun.
The Hokies then called Gobblers, victors 1960 and '66 were the years;
1970 Charlie Richards leads the Spiders, puts Pirates on their rears.
Much jubilation accompanied the stellar Tobacco Bowl event,
The number of fans who packed the stadium seemed Heaven sent.
All good things will have to end or so the stories told,
Oh not this, our Richmond's Gem, the storied Tobacco Bowl?
Will fate step in and silence our stadium's majestic roar,
Was Mr. Poe envisioning our bowl in his verse, "Nevermore"?

The Tobacco Bowl

October 15, 1949, VMI Victory Over Spiders Highlights Gala First Festival, 14-7

A new chapter in Richmond's football history was imminent with its first annual Collegiate Tobacco Bowl Festival, a gala four-day program featuring radio shows, appearances by Frank Sinatra, parades, crowning of Tobacco Bowl Queen and the prestigious football game. This inaugural gridiron contest pitted our Richmond Spiders, led by head coach Dick Esleeck, against the Virginia Military Institute Keydets and their head coach Tom Nugent. The Lexington Keydets marched to victory behind their field general, Joe Veltri, who tossed two touchdown passes, and a stubborn VMI defensive unit which had a pair of second half goal line stands. The Keydets were led by glue-fingered receivers Red Patton and Tommy Birge, who each scored on touchdown passes, and the defensive stars Bill Lauerman, Charlie Schluter and team Captain Tom Phillips. Richmond's battle-scarred tailback Cotton Billingsley suffered a game ending injury late in the second period and did not return to the contest. This injury to Richmond's star back seemed to seal the Spider's fate and many thought cost them the game.

OCTOBER 15, 1949, DOROTHY KIRSTEN "KICKS OFF" TOBACCO BOWL
As "Grand Marshall" Frank Sinatra cautiously spots the football, Tobacco Bowl Queen Dorothy Kirsten gingerly approaches the pigskin to kick off the Tobacco Bowl Festival. The pair of nationally renowned singers were the star attractions for the 1949 event and added a seductive ambience to the Tobacco Bowl and the other pageantry accompanying the occasion. As a sidenote, just after Kirsten kicked the pigskin, Sinatra quipped to a reporter, "I'm rootin' for VMI." (Photo by Louis Patterson and is from the collection of Buddy & Jimmy Patterson)

The Tobacco Bowl

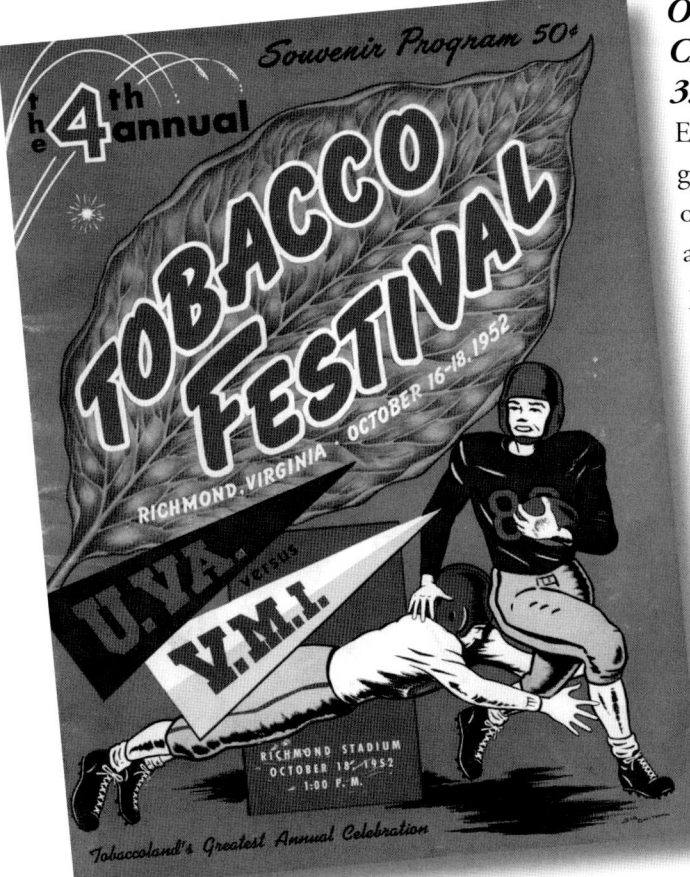

October 18, 1952, Cavaliers Crush Keydets 33-14

Eddie Knowles, the little all-the-way guy, lit a fire under the University of Virginia late in the third quarter and set off a chain reaction which produced a 33-14 Cavalier victory over an aggressive VMI squad. Knowles 58 yard punt return touchdown scamper was aided by murderous blocking and spine-tingling moves as he came home "tightrope walking" the sidelines. Richmond's own Tom Ford, the Cavalier defensive captain, provided special excitement with bone-chilling, fumble-causing tackles. A ray of sunshine for the Keydets was provided by George Chumbley, the elusive running back out of Thomas Jefferson High School, who had a crowd pleasing 32 yard scamper. This fourth annual Tobacco Festival game provided much pageantry and entertainment, including a real live tobacco auction, a fleet of antique automobiles, four bands, fancy floats, and the concession stands ran out of cold drinks before kick off.

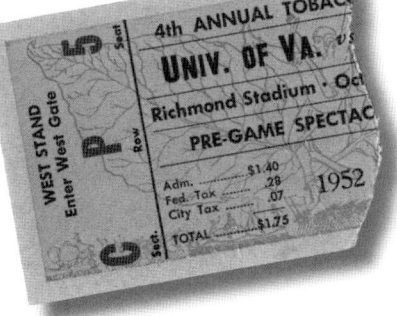

George Chumbley

Football in Richmond

ALEX HAWKINS

October 13, 1956, Gamecocks and "Captain Who" Down Cavaliers 27-13

Down 13-0, The University of Virginia's battered football team emerged from halftime charging the field with determination. After Coach Ben Martin's peppery halftime speech, the Cavaliers responded in the third quarter by playing an aggressive, inspired brand of football, while managing to tie the score 13-13 early in the fourth quarter. This is when South Carolina's stable of outstanding running backs took over, led by Alex Hawkins, who scored two of the Gamecocks' touchdowns. Hawkins, a "whirling dervish" type of player went on to a ten year NFL career with the Baltimore Colts and Atlanta Falcons, while obtaining the nickname "Captain Who" from Dick Butkus.

The Tobacco Bowl

October 17, 1959, VPI and Eastman Roll Over Virginia 40-14

On this "Chamber of Commerce" sunny afternoon, before a Tobacco Festival crowd of 24,000, hometown hero Frank Eastman led the VPI Gobblers to a convincing victory over the Virginia Cavaliers. Eastman, out of Hermitage High School, was at the controls for the first four VPI touchdowns, including two touchdown passes. His valiant play and daring field generalship led Head Coach Frank Moseley to say, "It looks as if the Gobblers have themselves a new #1 quarterback." Also providing outstanding performances were the gifted runner, Alger Pugh and All-American candidate Carroll Dale, who threw key blocks bowling over Cavalier defenders. And the Highty Tighties band tooted the victory song.

FRANK EASTMAN

Football in Richmond

October 24, 1970, Spiders Led By Richards Breeze Over ECU 38-12

With new Tobacco Bowl Queen Brenda Childress looking on and our Richmond Spiders exulting Coach Frank Jones' "locker room psychology," the team breezed to a 38-12 victory in the 22nd Tobacco Festival Game. Led by their charismatic quarterback Charlie Richards, who tossed the pigskin for over 200 yards and 3 touchdowns, the Spiders forced many Pirate mistakes and capitalized on them quickly. The play of the game was a dazzling 83 yard interception return for a touchdown by Richmond's Wayne Tosh. Our sticky-fingered receivers, Jerry Haynes and Jim Livesay, brought the stadium crowd to their feet more than once with their circus catches and elusive moves. The Spider defense was led by All-Southern Conference tackles John Barelli and Bruce Kasarda.

CHARLIE RICHARDS

1967 RICHMOND MUSTANGS

A team photo of our Richmond Mustangs gives flesh to the awesome statistics compiled by the team in the fall of 1967. This fraternity of football elite possessed an explosive arsenal of talent, while scoring a record 839 points, which stood as a minor league football season scoring record. The Mustangs averaged 64.5 points per game and received recognition from the national news media and Sports Illustrated. The team is flanked by Head Coach Dick James and Owner Hal Shapiro.

SECOND QUARTER
RICHMOND MUSTANGS 1967

New owner, coach and league for the season of '67,
We'll call our team the Mustangs, an awesome football eleven.
Dick James our head coach, ex-star of the Washington Redskins,
Will his expertise and experience produce a champion with wins?
Few could imagine the amount of points this team would score,
There was 105 against Savannah, against Boston 92 more.
Merv Holland and Donald Redford, quite efficient tossing the ball
To Robbins, Barber and Adams, to the goal line they did haul.
Rushers Herman, McWatters and Carter, with that pig's bladder they did run
McNeill, Whittier and Hamilton our blockers, man this scoring was fun.
A team that lacked a defense, could not have won a game
Led by Appler, Duty, Fleming and Christman, Mustangs defensive Hall of Fame.
And then safety Lloyd Swelnis, his interceptions, quite a ball hawk
Also returned our punts, left the opposition in the dark.
Bill Joyner was the kicker, booted them way out of sight
Led the league in scoring, his PATs split the uprights.
Mustangs averaged 64 points, opponents they did kill
But soon they would swallow the proverbial bitter pill
With scores like 85-0, the league teams they did trounce
Our players surprised in October, when their paychecks began to bounce
Owner Shapiro says he's busted, players vote, they won't play
November 1st car magnet Bill Templeton, comes forth to save the day
New owner, new name, Richmond Roadrunners, we now will be called
Will the players be the same, the fans want to see more football
Next game against Pennsylvania, would this Roadrunner become our hero
Team steps up and mauls the Marauders, score was 72 to zero.
This fall filled with touchdowns and turmoil throughout the year
Our players fought through adversity, on the gridiron had no peer.
Two names in one season, Mustangs-Roadrunners they scored a ton
The championship belonged to Richmond, with a record of 12-1.

Mustangs Brain Trust

Pictured above is the coaching staff of the Richmond Mustangs. This group of genuinely dedicated footballers were coaches both on and off the field. The "brain trust" helped produce an avalanche of touchdowns and a defense that would make the Gipper proud, all of which culminated in a championship season. Pictured: (l-r) Doug McNeill, Dick James, Jim Rossi, and Don Christman.

Lloyd Swelnis

A two-way performer at Western Michigan University with All-Mid-American Conference honors, Lloyd roamed the defensive backfield for the Rebels, Mustangs and Roadrunners. With the Mustangs he was one of the league leaders in both interceptions and punt returns. The spark plug of the defense, his nose for the ball had him leading the team in interceptions. As a punt returner, his shifty running often left opponents out to dry, while performing for this Wonder Team of 1967.

Richmond Mustang Defense 1967
The gridiron became a temple for this group of spirited, red-blooded defensive football players. Both physically aggressive and possessing an enthusiasm that was contagious, the Mustangs defense pitched one shutout after another while performing pleasantly rough recreation with the opponent's running backs. Pictured: Kneeling (l-r) Ray Creasy, Hugh Watkins, Peter Alfred, Gene Appler; Center Row (l-r) Henry Jones, Don Christman, Ron Fleming; Back Row (l-r) Ray Dark, Jim Rossi, Lloyd Swelnis, Bob Tyrus.

Merv Holland
Quarterback extraordinaire, Merv epitomized a winner as he led the Mustangs with his leadership ability and accurate passing game in the season of 1967. Possessing all the requisites of a good quarterback, Merv had numerous prodigious passing performances throughout the season, even though he was pulled early from many games due to the lopsided score. And did you really draw up some plays in the huddle?

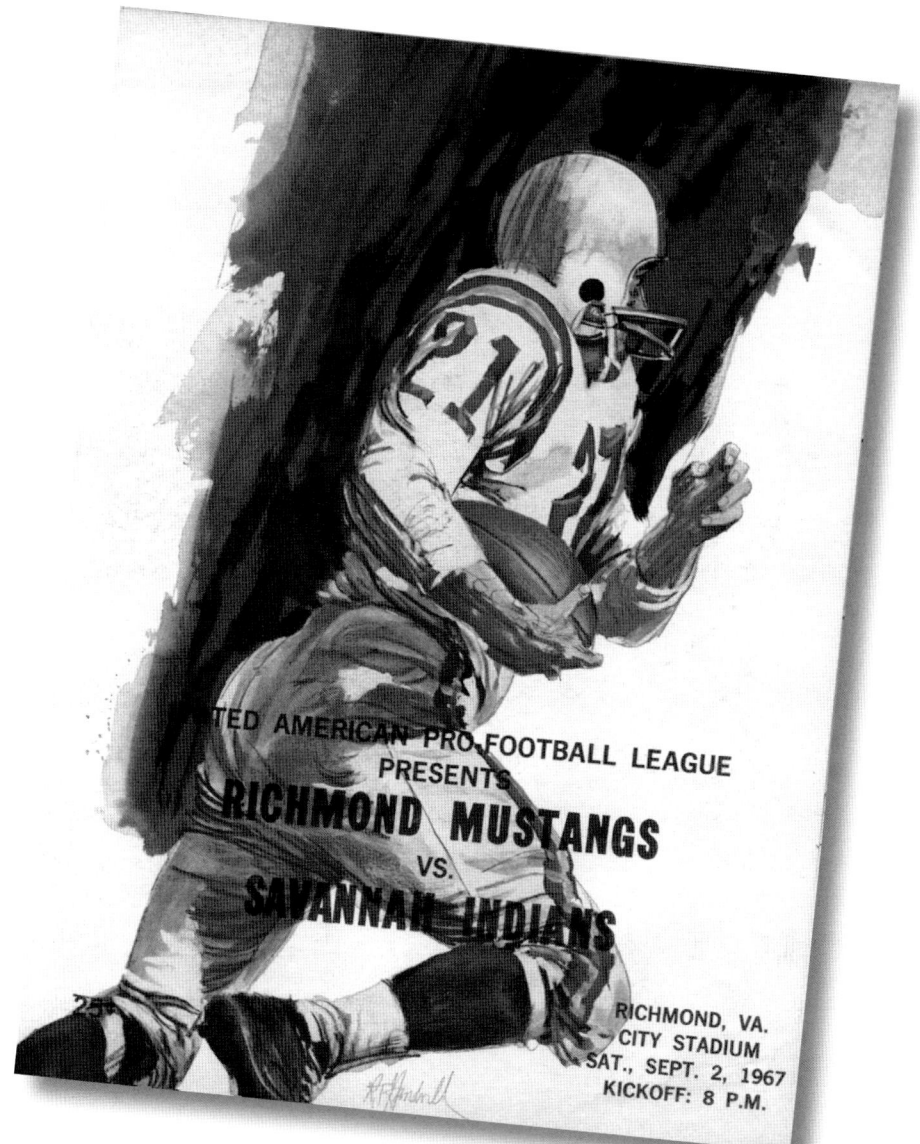

RICHMOND VS SAVANNAH, SEPTEMBER 2, 1967, "AND THE SCORE WAS..."
One of the most historic programs in Richmond's football history is displayed here. Our Richmond Mustangs, on this warm September evening at City Stadium, annihilated our visitors from Georgia by a score of 105-0. This lopsided victory by our Mustangs vaulted the Richmond team to national fame. With seven touchdown passes by Merv Holland and Don Redford, and Bill Joyner's 15 PATs, the team rewrote numerous offensive records. On defense the Mustangs were equally adept, as our goal line remained unviolated and linebacker Red Christman returned two pass interceptions for touchdowns. And the 6,400 fans were still buzzing long after the final gun sounded.

Student Body Left

Led by pulling guards Doug McNeill #66 (George Washington University) and Henry Hamilton #64 (Virginia Union University), Charlie Herman #48 circles left end on one of his many touchdown jaunts in 1967. Herman, a 190 pounder, was a dynamo as a running back for the Mustangs. Both McNeill and Hamilton as pulling guards created headaches for defenses in this storybook season of 1967.

Jake Adams

A bull of strength for the Mustangs, Jake, out of Highland Springs High School and Virginia Tech, was arguably one of the top tight ends in the league in the 1967 season. At 6'5" and 240 pounds, this mountain of a man made many a defender pay the price while attempting to bring him to the ground. Known for his fierce competitive spirit, he also starred for the 1966 Rebels and the Roadrunners. Drafted by the NFL's St. Louis Cardinals, Jake also played briefly with the Kansas City in the AFL.

Richmond Mustangs

Bill Joyner

Bill "The Booter" Joyner stood 5'11" and weighed in at 255 pounds during his playing days with the Richmond Rebels and the Mustangs. As the kicker for the Mustangs in 1967, he split the uprights on 117 extra points and 11 field goals for a total of 140 points, which still stands as the scoring record for a kicker in Minor League Football. Known as the "Cadillac" of kickers, Bill was selected to the All-Star team while playing for the Rebels in 1966.

Dave Robbins

This 5'11", 185 pound flanker out of Catawba College was an integral part of the Mustang's offense. One of the teams scoring and reception leaders, it was said of Dave that he "catches passes the way the rest of us catch the common cold." After snaring the elongated sphere from the air, he electrified players and spectators with his pursuit to the end zone. Created for leadership, Dave, post Mustangs, became the illustrious head basketball coach of the Virginia Union University Panthers.

GENE APPLER AND LLOYD SWELNIS- LEADERS

The photographer at old City Stadium has captured a priceless moment of these two charismatic Richmond Mustang football players. As leaders of our 1967 footballers, both Gene and Lloyd were immensely popular players who brought dignity to the game of football. Their play on the gridiron was characterized with the "passion and desire" they brought to the sport. Respected not only for their legendary accomplishments on the football field, but also for their accomplishments in the game of life. The spirit of the 1967 Mustangs is fully expressed in this photo.

TOROS VS MUSTANGS, NOVEMBER 23, 1967 - "VENDETTA" VICTORY

An extremely rare and significant ticket stub from Richmond's football past, this stub was for a "vendetta" game against the San Antonio Toros played on Thanksgiving Day 1967. The Toros were the only team to beat our Mustangs in this historic season, by a score of 10-9 earlier in the season. Our Mustangs came out victorious on this day by pasting the Toros 30-7 and Coach Dick James boasted, "I never had any doubts we could do it." (Note: By this date the Richmond team had changed their nickname to Roadrunners, the Toros botched this also, as the ticket reads Richmond, Virginia Mustangs.)

Artifacts & Memorabilia

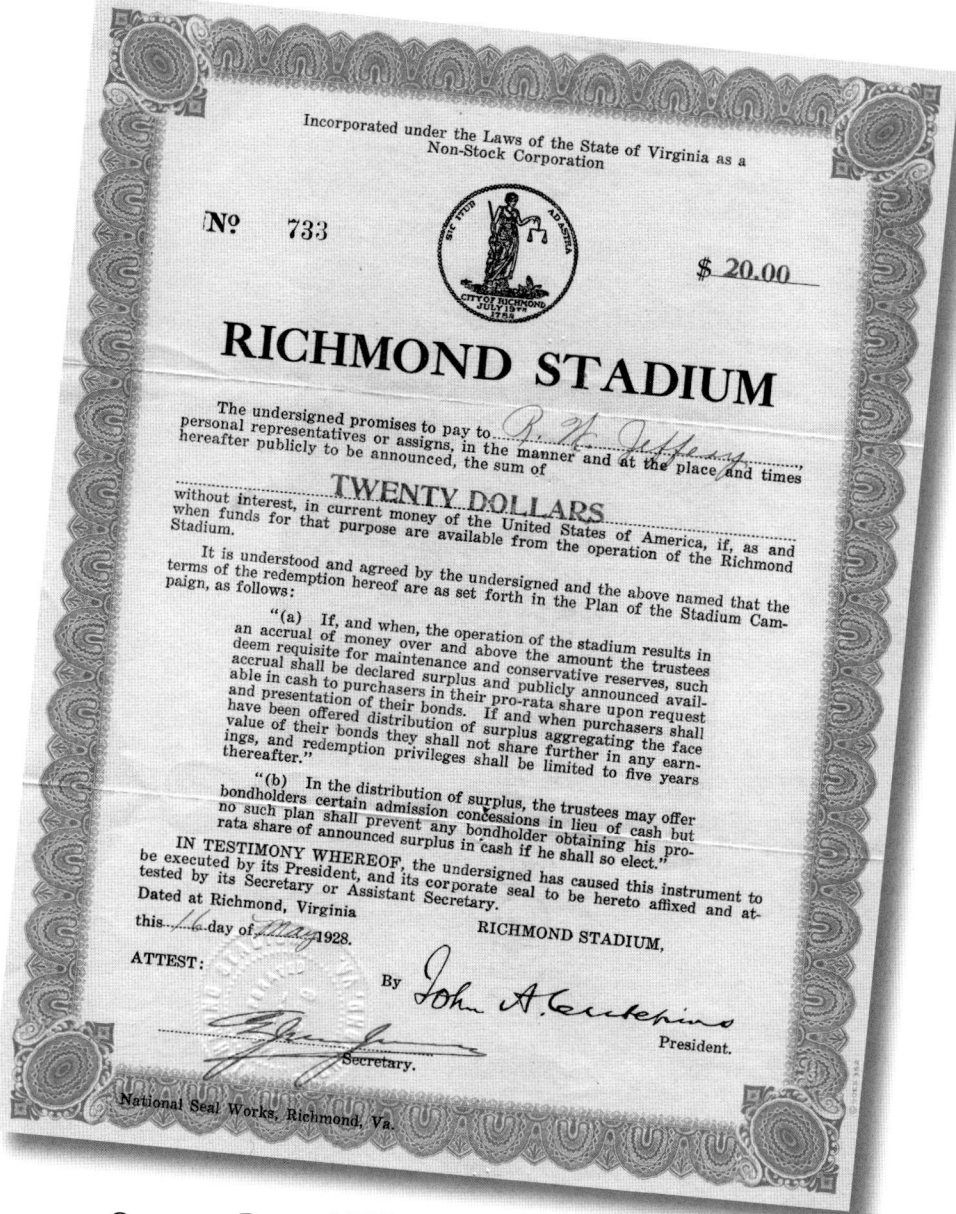

Richmond Stadium Bond 1928

Storied and historically important to the resurgence of football as a "main event" on our Richmond sports scene, were these bonds for the Richmond Stadium. This particular bond for twenty dollars has elaborately engraved orange borders, the embossed "Richmond Stadium" corporate seal affixed at bottom left and dated May 16, 1928. With the official dedication of the stadium in November 1929, our Richmond Arrows will find a new place to call home. This bond is an exceptional piece of Richmond's football history.

HALFTIME
ARTIFACTS & MEMORABILIA

The teams oh so many, the player oh so fine
Which have truly left their marks, since that season of '29.
Started out as Richmond Arrows, ended up as the Saints,
Rebels, Roadrunners, Mustangs; our city they would paint
The fans came in flocks, many tickets there was sold
To see the JM-TJ classic, and also the Tobacco Bowl
And while we're talking classic, let's not forget at all
The teams coached by Maxie, and "The Cannonball".
Sammy Baugh brought his Championship Redskins in the season of '38
With his running and his passing, he quickly sealed their fate.
In '39 Walt Kiesling brought his Pirates, to play on a dare
Not to be outdone, in 1950 George Halas brought his Bears.
The college teams also came, many seats they did fill
Half left happy, half were sad; as told by the scoreboard on the hill.
Not a coliseum or field covered with a dome,
But the Spiders felt comfortable in calling this football field home.
Nestled in the corner of McCloy and Maplewood,
This stadium of ours, in a small town neighborhood.
Fond memories we shall keep, the thrills much the same,
This River City shrine, where football was the game.
And when the final whistle blows, and from the press box there's no sound,
Remember our City Stadium, a gem in Richmond's crown!

Artifacts & Memorabilia

Executioner Style Football Helmet

This gridiron relic that's as archaic as they come was popular during the 1920s. It was called "The Executioner" because the leather helmet extended to cover all of the face with holes for the eyes, nose and mouth. This extremely scarce and desirable item has the Spalding logo stamped on the forehead. There are few football helmets of this caliber in existence today. Could this unique piece have been worn by one of our own Richmond Arrow football stars at old Hotchkiss Field?

Football in Richmond

Tony Gallovich - Richmond Rebels Jersey

This game jersey, truly a piece of Richmond football legacy, was worn by Tony Gallovich, a premier running back for the Rebels in the mid to late 1940s. Gallovich had starred at Wake Forest University and the Cleveland Rams of the NFL. The durene jersey has sewn on red felt numerals and embedded elbow reinforcements, with a number of repairs consistent with the many times Tony toted the pigskin at old City Stadium.

Tobacco Festival "Official" Badge 1950s

A fabulous and rare example of an "officials" pinback badge for the Tobacco Festival's football game. This unique treasure features a football player between two large tobacco leaves, with print "Official Tobacco Festival." Measuring 2 1/4" in diameter, the brown and gold boldly colored pinback pridefully preserves the memories of the Tobacco Bowl, an integral part of Richmond's football past.

Artifacts & Memorabilia

Turkey Day Program

This beautiful relic from a bygone era in Richmond's football history is from a game on Thanksgiving Day 1925. This gridiron classic was played at the "historic" Mayo Island Park and pitted the University of Richmond footballers against William & Mary. The program contains superb player and Richmond team photos, along with pics of Spider's Coach Dobson and Indian's "Chief" Tasker. Fabulous period ads are displayed throughout and, by the way, William & Mary blanked the Spider eleven on this Thanksgiving Day 14-0.

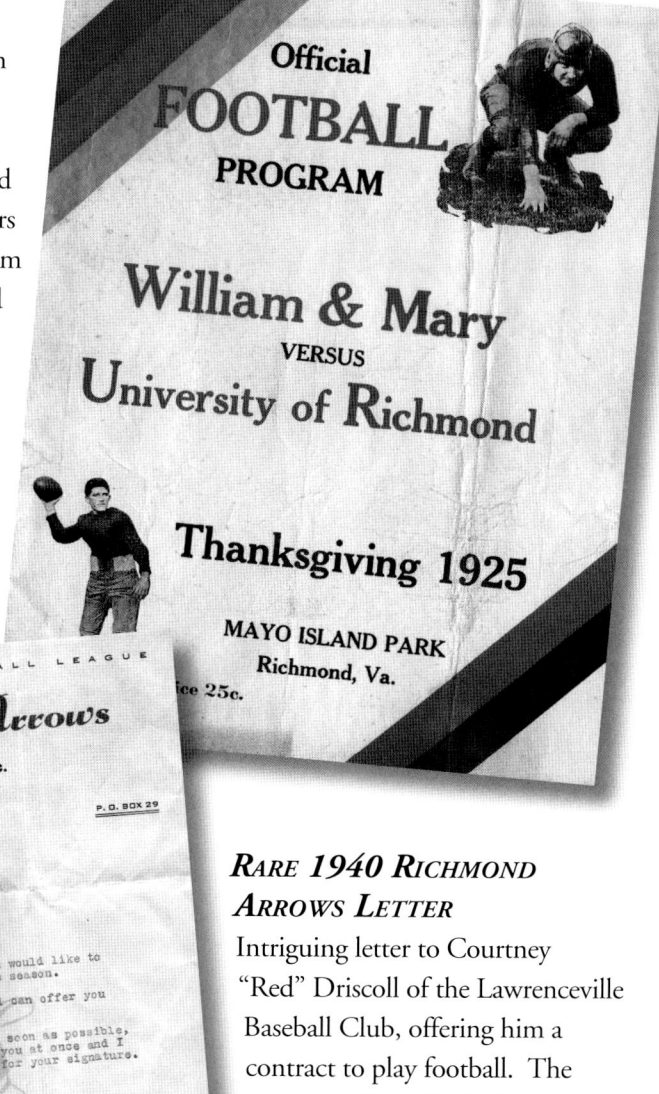

Rare 1940 Richmond Arrows Letter

Intriguing letter to Courtney "Red" Driscoll of the Lawrenceville Baseball Club, offering him a contract to play football. The contract offer is for $15.00 per game, and is typed neatly on The Richmond Arrows letterhead, dated August 12, 1940 and signed by the Arrow's General Manager Linwood Jones. This is quite a unique piece of Richmond football history.

ARROW ATHLETIC CLUB vs MARYLAND ATHLETIC CLUB 1935 PROGRAM

This rare gem found tucked away in someone's dresser drawer contains a juggernaut of Richmond Arrow history. Crackerjack photos of Arrow players, accolades on past and present players, a history of the Arrow Athletic Club, bio of Head Coach Dave Miller, team rosters with starting lineups, graphic merchant advertising and an article, which I found most amusing; "How to Choose Your Football Girl." Truly tangible evidence of our Arrow footballers from the 1930s.

RICHMOND ARROW VS PITTSBURGH PIRATES 1939 FULL TICKET

The "crown jewel" for ticket collectors is to find an unused vintage full ticket, and does this one fit the bill. This vintage full ticket was for a game at Richmond Stadium, on November 12, 1939, pitting our Arrow team against the Pittsburgh Pirates. The Pirates walloped the Arrows 33-0. This historical ticket of Richmond's football past would dazzle even the novice of ticket collector.

Artifacts & Memorabilia

Fred Cooper Day Football, November 13, 1949

Fred "Cannonball" Cooper showcased his mythical talents as a player during the Richmond Rebels championship seasons of 1949 and 1950. During the 1949 season the Rebel organization and our Richmond "footballites" organized a Fred Cooper Day. The football seen here is one of the many awards and gifts presented to Cannonball on this historic day. Printed on the white game football is; " To: Fred "Cannonball" Cooper, A Great Football Player and Gentleman From: The Richmond Rebels November 13, 1949". This historical football occupies a premier place in this author's trophy room.

Matchbook Schedule – 1948

Vintage piece of Richmond's football past, a rare matchbook cover of Rebels home game schedule for the season of 1948 at Richmond's City Stadium. Cover states "Root for the Rebels" with a caricature of a player punting the football. Could this have been our star kicker Glenn Knox?

Football in Richmond

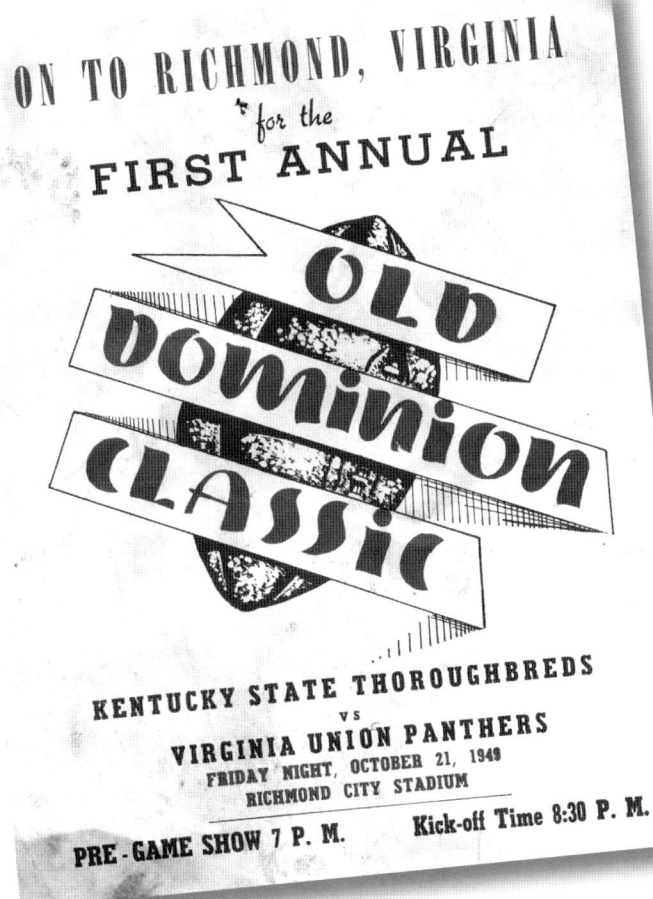

Old Dominion Classic 1949 Virginia Union Panthers

Phenomenal football program from the first annual "Old Dominion Classic" played at Richmond's City Stadium. This magnificent relic pays homage to the legendary football program at Virginia Union University. In this gridiron tilt the Panthers upset the multi-talented Thoroughbreds of Kentucky State by a score of 27-14. This vintage program also encourages spectators to view the "animated" Union Panther and the high stepping pretty majorettes cutting their cakewalk capers. After the game there was a "Victory Dance" at the Atlantic Rural Exposition.

University of Richmond Pinback 1950

If you have an appetite for mementos, then this vintage pinback from the University of Richmond homecoming football game in 1950 is the relic for you. Colorful Spider logo graphic, flaunting its original luster with "helmeted" Spider in his passing pose. Two inches in diameter, the souvenir keepsake was probably purchased from one of the vendors at old City Stadium.

Artifacts & Memorabilia

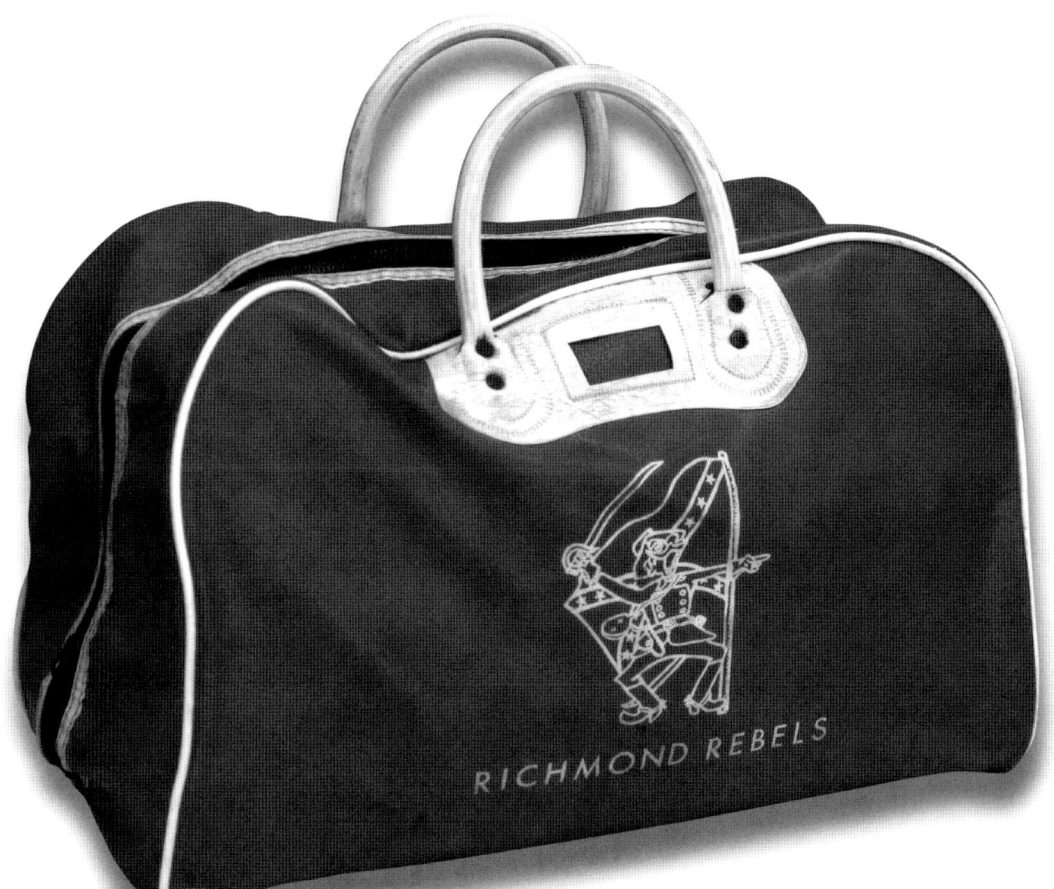

Richmond Rebels Carry Bag

Here is a vintage 1964 Richmond Rebels player carry bag featuring the sword swinging soldier and Confederate flag logo on the bag's side panel. Red with white trim and measuring 10" X 17", this zippered travel bag most likely carried the player's most prized possessions. This is truly a seldom seen piece of Richmond's football past.

Rubber Nose Guard 1890-1920

An extremely rare keepsake from football's turn of the century is seen here. This hard rubber nose guard featured breathing holes, elastic strap and mouthpiece to aid in securement. Long since discarded due to breathing difficulty and bulkiness, the nose guard was regarded as "standard" equipment in the 1890s.

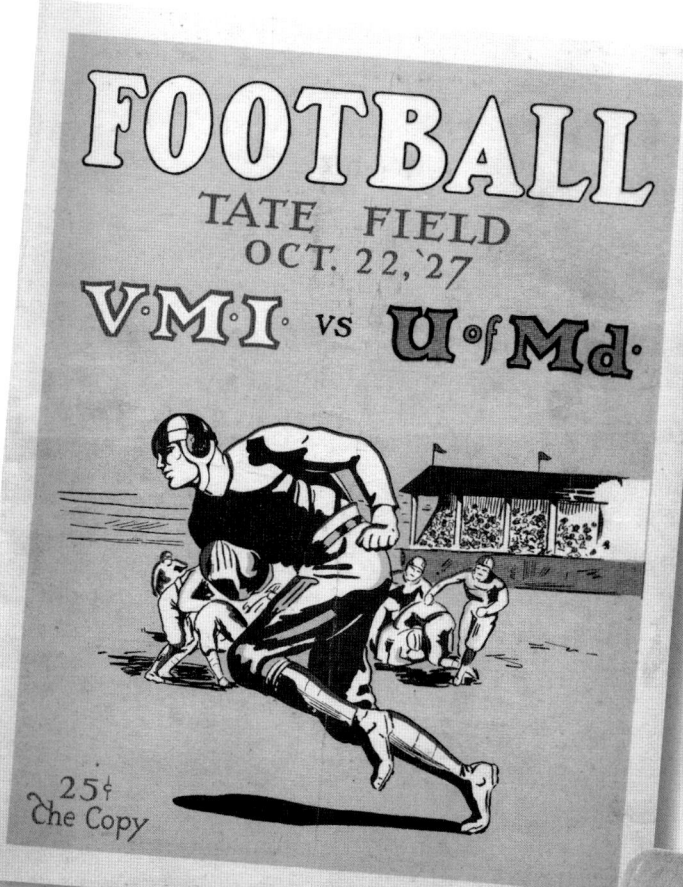

Football Program Tate Field 1927

This official program hails from the October 22, 1927 contest between Virginia Military Institute and the University of Maryland. The game was played at Tate Field, which was named for Richmond baseball great "Pop" Tate. The souvenir program was creatively produced by the V.M.I. Club of Richmond and boasts player rosters, two pictures depicting each team's captain, starting lineups, team yells and songs, along with artistic advertising.

Rare Cigarette Case 1951 Tobacco Festival

A most sentimental and enduring memento of Richmond's Tobacco Festival is this plastic cigarette case imprinted "Third Annual Tobacco Festival October 8th-13th"; also imprinted "Retail Merchant's Day October 8th." Measuring 2 1/2" X 3" this rare item truly symbolizes the spirit of which the Tobacco Festival stood.

ARTIFACTS & MEMORABILIA

RARE RICHMOND REBELS CHEERLEADER UNIFORM

This riveting relic was worn on the sidelines of the Richmond Rebels by one of their cheerleaders. The white corduroy garment features red piping and the Rebels sequined "R" on the front with a zipper back. Not much material to this one, which was probably to the liking of the players and fans, as they cheered the team to victory, "Sis-Boom-Ba!" (From the wardrobe of ex-Rebel cheerleader Susan Johnson)

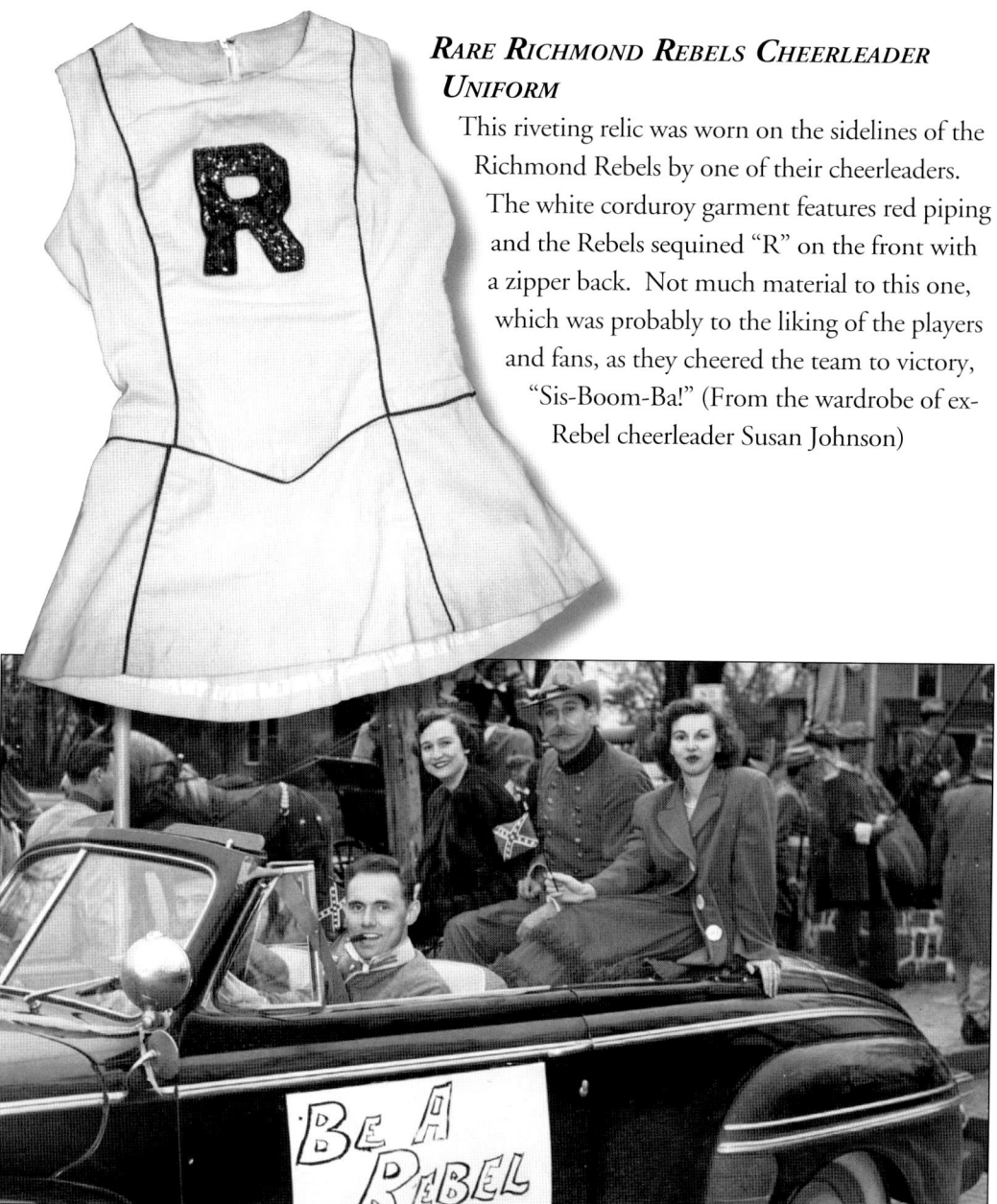

RICHMOND REBELS PARADE

"Be a Rebel," as the message on the side of this vintage convertible shouts to the parade attendees. A pre-season celebration to inspire enthusiasm for the upcoming football season, the parade produced a myriad of Rebel charismatic players decked out in Civil War period Confederate uniforms. One of the heroes of the day, riding on the back of an auto surrounded by two beautiful ladies, is none other than that legendary Richmond footballer, Chester Fritz.

Football in Richmond

Richmond Rebels Full Ticket 1964

This full unused ticket for our Rebels is as flawless as the fond memories provided by the footballers in the season of 1964. Measuring 1 1/2" by 3 1/2", ticket was for general admission in the west stand and cost $2.00. With Pete Pihos as their leader, the Rebels emerged with the reputation of a winner going undefeated in their final seven games of the season and again brought this fall spectacle to the forefront for Richmond football fans.

Richmond Rebels Game Worn Jersey 1964

Finding one of these game worn Rebels jerseys is about as rare as a lobster dinner. This vintage durene jersey was made by Southern Athletic Manufacturing Company and features a v-neck with three stripes adorning the shoulder yoke and sleeves. The numerals are sewn on and made of tackle twill. Battle-scarred and showing extensive signs of game use and wear with dirt from City Stadium caked into the fabric. Ted Denby, a 6'1", 200 pound halfback out of the University of Virginia, is listed in a 1964 program as the wearer of #32.

Artifacts & Memorabilia

Tobacco Bowl Football Award Charm 1946

A most sentimental and enduring memento from a landmark event in Richmond's football history. Twenty-two players smashed and slammed each other until time was called and the scoreboard read 6-6. This historic game pitted the high schoolers from Glen Allen against Highland Springs in the Tobacco Bowl Classic played at City Stadium, December 7, 1946. This gold plated Tobacco Bowl charm was presented to the defensive standout Bill Cooley and proudly displays the date and initials B.C.

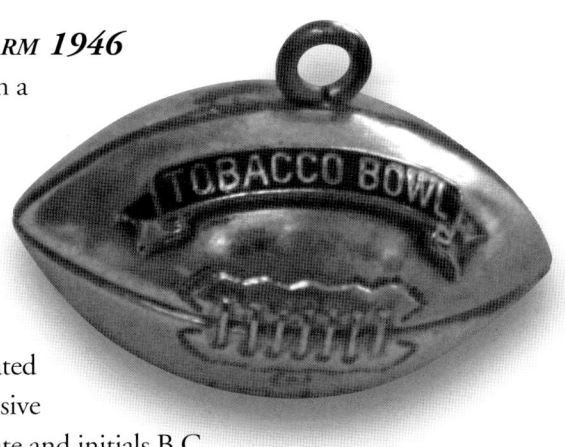

Richmond Rebels Letter 1950

Beautifully illustrated Richmond Rebels letterhead dated May 2, 1950. This visually pleasing piece from Richmond's football past also displays, "AMERICAN LEAGUE CHAMPIONS 1949"! Letter content pertains to "gold footballs" which are still on order and team-player pictures. Very attractive two page letter, which is signed by team president, H. C. Seibold.

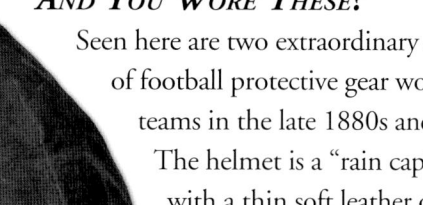

AND YOU WORE THESE?

Seen here are two extraordinary examples of football protective gear worn by teams in the late 1880s and 1890s. The helmet is a "rain cap" style with a thin soft leather outer shell, while the interior is lined in heavy felt. The ear protection hung loose over the ears. The shoulder pads also composed of leather and lined with felt were often worn on the exterior, lying flat on the shoulders and strapped under the arms. These pads possess a vintage Spalding logo.

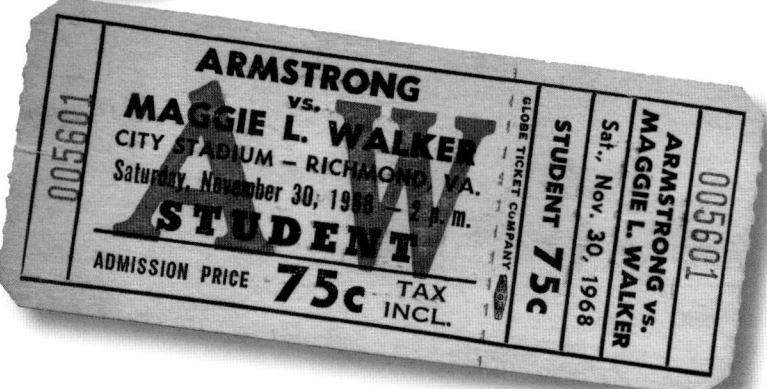

ARMSTRONG VS MAGGIE WALKER TICKET 1968

A mesmerizing piece of football memorabilia from the historic classic football game featuring Armstrong High School against Maggie Walker High School. The football relic delivers a very vintage appeal for this student admission of seventy-five cents. There was happiness aplenty on the Maggie Walker sidelines as the Green Dragons smashed the Wildcats by a score of 18-8.

Artifacts & Memorabilia

Rare Toros vs Mustangs 1967 Program

The program heading tells it all, "Rematch of the Decade." Our nationally acclaimed Richmond Mustangs, who's only blemish on their schedule was a 10-9 defeat at the San Antonio Toros in October, traveled to San Antonio for this "Turkey Day Game" against the Toros who possessed an 18-0 record. Our Mustangs played valiantly, operating with a high powered offense and a salty defense completely overwhelmed the Toros as they exploded to a 30-7 "Vendetta" victory.

Richmond Roadrunners Mini Football

When Bill Templeton took over the ownership of the Richmond Mustangs late in the season of 1967, he realized that in order to get the "fannies in the stands" he needed to improve the promotional aspects of the game. One such promotion in the season of 1968 involved the tossing of mini-footballs into the stands by our sassy Richmond cheerleaders. Seen here is one of those balls speared by a lucky fan. The ball features the Richmond Roadrunners logo and Richmond Chrysler Plymouth Corporation, of which Templeton was the owner.

1950 Club Owner Pass

Wow!! Finding one of these is as rare as winning the lottery. American Football League 1950 season pass for the "Club Owner." This one was extended to Harry C. Seibold, our Richmond Rebels owner, "the courtesy of all its parks." Depicts the fantastic AFL logo, while the back lists the following league members: Bethlehem Bull-Dogs, Jersey City Giants, Paterson Panthers, Erie Vets, and Brooklyn.

Richmond Roadrunners Decal 1968

Pridefully displayed is this boldly colored decal from the old Richmond Roadrunners. This unique 4" X 4" decal is red, blue, yellow and white in colors, featuring the Roadrunners logo and the Atlantic Coast Football League logo. Some fan failed to apply this decal to their auto back window during our season of 1968.

─── ARTIFACTS & MEMORABILIA ───

RICHMOND SAINTS BALLPOINT PEN

This unique relic from Richmond's football past features the Saints home schedule at Richmond's City Stadium for the season of 1970. The black and white ballpoint pen also depicts the team's logo and was made by Tucker. Only a handful of these rare pieces are known to exist.

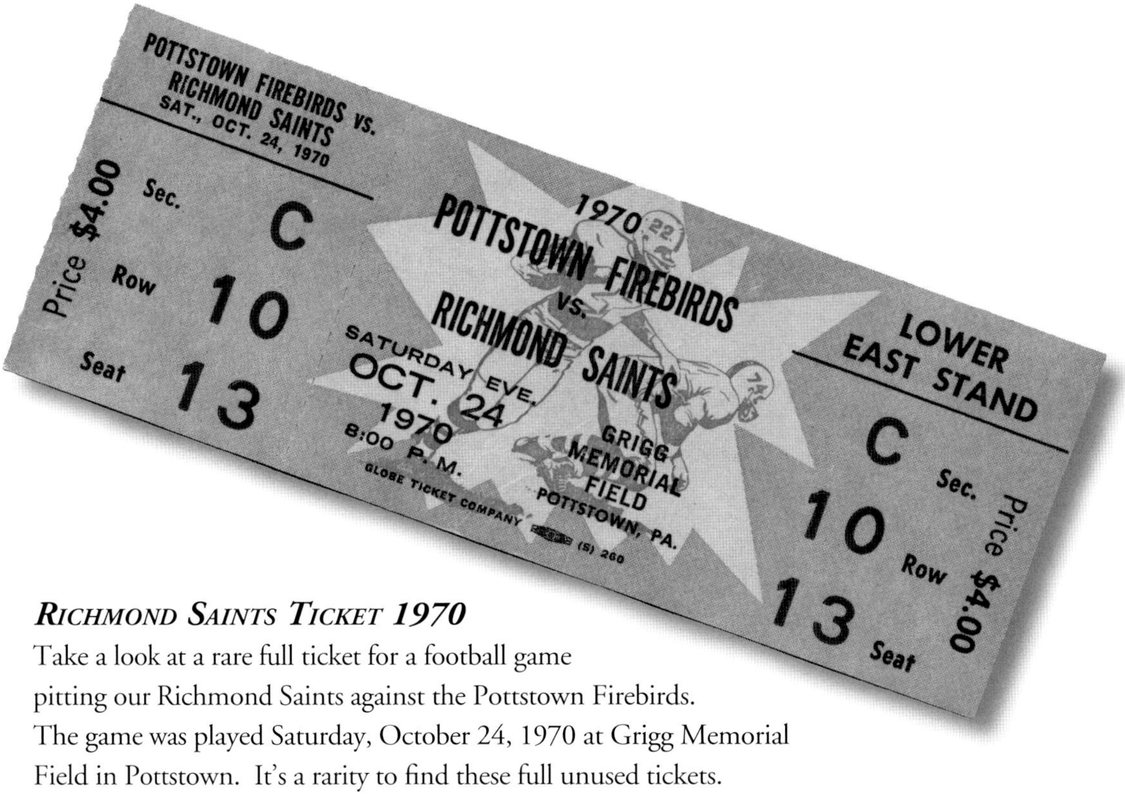

RICHMOND SAINTS TICKET 1970

Take a look at a rare full ticket for a football game pitting our Richmond Saints against the Pottstown Firebirds. The game was played Saturday, October 24, 1970 at Grigg Memorial Field in Pottstown. It's a rarity to find these full unused tickets.

THE AMERICAN FOOTBALL LEAGUE

UNIFORM PLAYER'S CONTRACT

The Richmond Rebels, Inc. herein called the Club,
and Chester Fritz herein called the Player, of 2700 Monument Ave., Richmond, Va.
Street City State

The Club is a member of *The American Football League*. As such, and jointly with the other members of the League it is obligated to insure to the public wholesome and high class professional football playing by defining the relation between Club and Player, and between Club and Club.

In view of the facts above recited the parties agree as follows:

1. The Club will pay the Player a salary for his skilled services during the playing season of 1950 at the rate of One Hundred ($100.00) dollars for each regularly scheduled League game played. For all other games the Player shall be paid no salary other than actual expenses.* As to games scheduled but not played, the Player shall receive no compensation from the Club other than actual expenses.

*This clause is changed to read as follows: Preseason exhibition games a salary of $25.00. Any exhibition game after season starts 50% of salary. If club makes the final play-off game the players of both teams receive the gate receipts less expenses of the League and both participating clubs as provided by the League by-laws.

2. The Player agrees that during said season he will faithfully serve the Club, and pledges himself to the American public to conform to high standards of fair play and good sportsmanship and will observe all player rules on reverse side of this contract.

3. The Player will not play football during 1950 otherwise than for the Club, except in case the Club shall have released said Player, and said release has been approved by the officials of *The American Football League*.

4. The Player accepts as part of this contract such reasonable regulations as the Club may announce from time to time.

5. This contract may be terminated at any time by the Club upon three (3) days' written notice to the Player.

6. The Player submits himself to the discipline of *The American Football League* and agrees to accept its decisions pursuant to its Constitution and By-Laws.

7. At any time prior to August 1st, 1951, by written notice to the Player, the Club may renew this contract for the term of that year, except that the salary rate shall be such as the parties may then agree upon, or in default of agreement, such as the Club may fix.

8. The Player may be fined or suspended for violation of this contract, but in all cases the Player shall have the right of appeal to the President of *The American Football League*.

9. In default of agreement the Player will accept the salary rate thus fixed or else will not play during said year otherwise than for the Club, unless the Club shall release the Player.

10. The reservation of the Club of the valuable right to fix the salary rate for the succeeding year, and the promise of the Player not to play during said year otherwise than with the Club, have been taken into consideration in determining the salary specified herein and the undertaking by the Club to pay said salary is the consideration for both the reservation and the promise.

11. In case of dispute between the Player and the Club, the same shall be referred to the President of *The American Football League*, and his decision shall be accepted by all parties as final.

12. Verbal contracts between Club and Player will not be considered by this Association, in the event of a dispute.

Signed this 24th day of July A. D. 1950

Witnesses:
R O Waldbauer
R. O. Waldbauer, Secretary

Richmond Rebels, Inc.
(Club)
By H. C. Seibold
H. C. Seibold, President and Treasurer
Chester Fritz (Player)

This copy is to be held by Player.

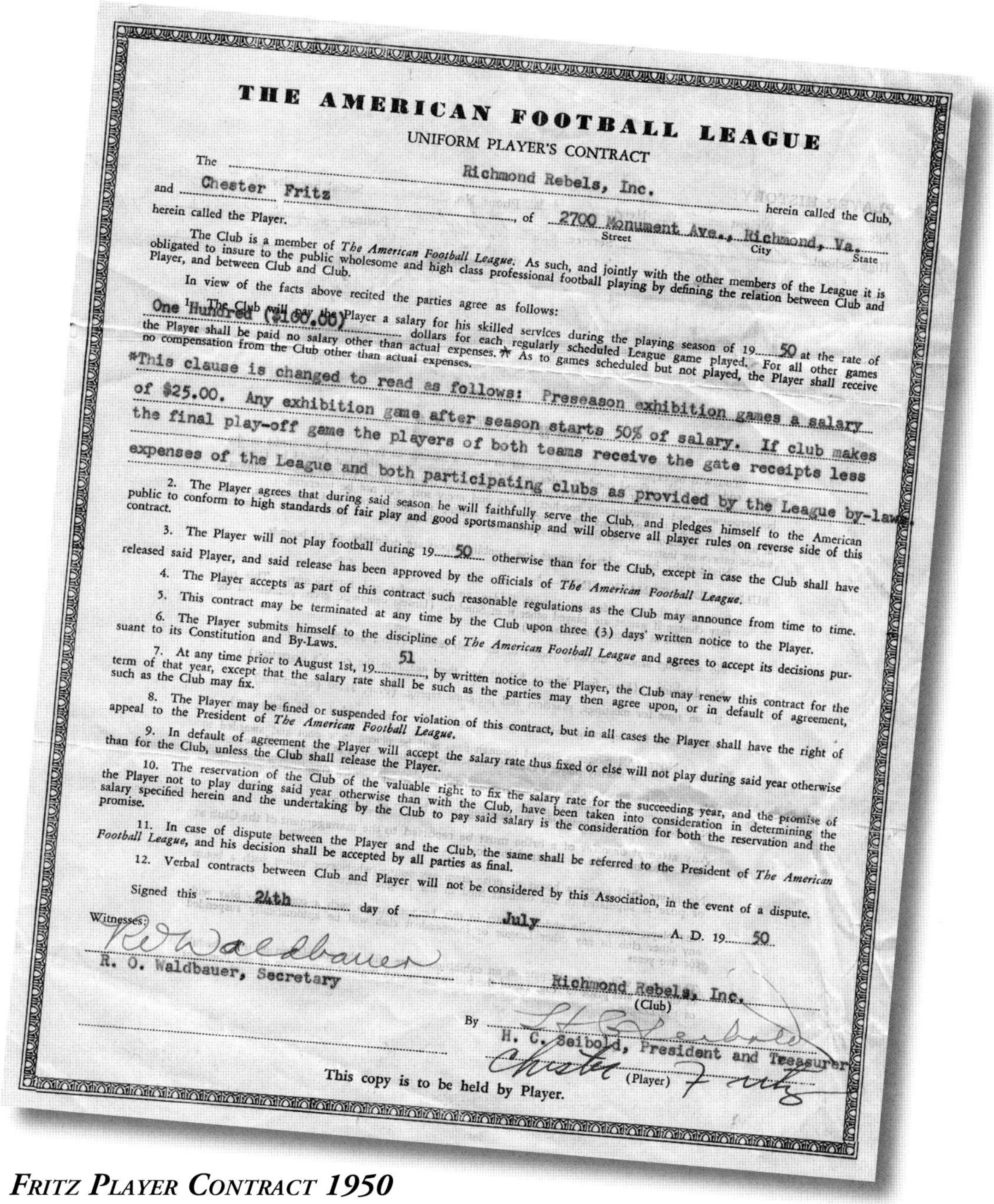

FRITZ PLAYER CONTRACT 1950

Displayed here is an American Football League uniform player's contract for Chester Fritz of the Richmond Rebels, Inc. "The Club will pay the player for his skilled services at the rate of one-hundred dollars for each regularly scheduled league game played, pre-season exhibition games a salary of $25.00." Contract is dated July 24, 1950 and signed by Fritz, President Seibold and Secretary Waldbauer. This is the only Rebels player's contract that the author has seen.

ROADRUNNERS AND SAINTS SIGN PACT

"It's official," on this late summer afternoon of 1968, our Richmond Roadrunners became an affiliate of the NFL's New Orleans Saints. A great day for pro-football here in the River City. Pictured, top row (l-r) the great Paul Hornung of Green Bay Packer fame, Richmond Owner Bill Templeton; bottom row (l-r) General Manager Gene Huggins, George Owens Assistant to the President of the New Orleans Saints

THIRD QUARTER
RICHMOND ROADRUNNERS 1968-1969

With the death of our Mustangs, in the winningest of years,
To our rescue Mr. Templeton and that Roadrunner appears.
Finishing the schedule, and forgiving past due sins,
This team now called Roadrunners close the season with 3 wins.
Templeton hard at work, joins ACFL for year of '68,
Fans just want more victories, wondering how this league will rate.
Diligently signing footballers, a slacker this man ain't;
Roadrunners sign a deal, an affiliate of New Orleans Saints.
With backing of the Saints, our talent should not lack
New Orleans sends Paul Hornung, to officially sign the pact.
Season quickly approaching, how would our Roadrunners fair
Sign Duke's Al Woodall, to toss the pigskin through the air;
Rossi, Robbins and Barber, many veterans return this fall
Even Coach Dick James, will be running the oblong ball.
But the opponent's goal line, seldom did we cross
And few touchdown passes did our quarterbacks toss.
With the season now over, all's said and done
The Roadrunners record was 4-7-1.
Many new faces and new unis for season of '69
Signs J. D. Roberts to coach, a master of the line
An eighteen year old running sensation, namely Ike Brown
Leads the ACFL in rushing, and claims the leagues crown.
As the year progressed, the team seemed to jive,
Our Roadrunners end the season, winning 7 and losing 5!

DICK JAMES – HEAD COACH
MUSTANGS AND ROADRUNNERS

Versatility and the ability to inspire were the trademarks of this NFL veteran, who coached both our Richmond Mustangs and Roadrunners. As a star player for the Washington Redskins, James specialized in kickoff and punt returns, while also playing defensive wingback and safety. In 1961, he was named the "Redskin Player of the Year." Known as a fierce competitor, James is the only player in NFL history ever to win the MVP voting both offensively and defensively in the same game, September 28, 1958. As coach of our Mustangs/Roadrunners of 1967, Dick had a succession of triumphs with a championship season of twelve victories and only 1 defeat.

Henry Hamilton

Producing the effects of a steamroller for our Mustangs and Roadrunners, this star guard was an integral part of the success of our Richmond teams. At 6'2", 240 pounds, "Hank" was an All-C.I.A.A. performer at Virginia Union University. He also had a "cup of coffee" with the Buffalo Bills and the Toronto Rifles. Possessing a true passion for the game, Henry also served as the offensive line coach for the Roadrunners.

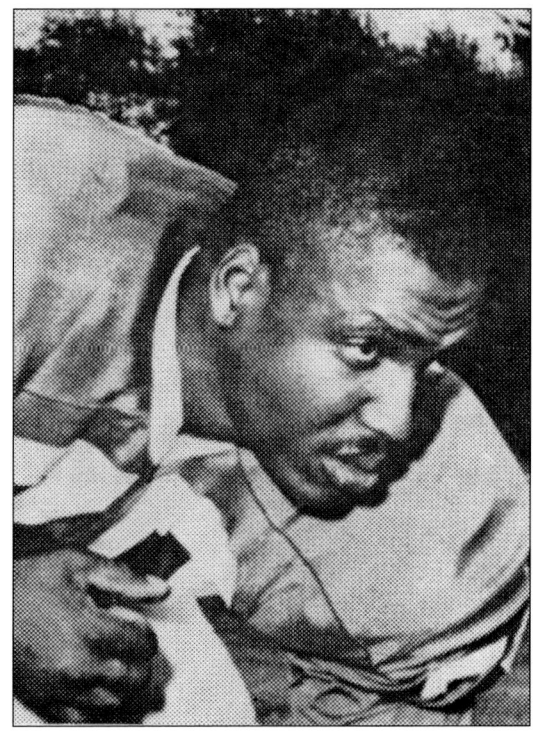

Avery Sumner

The pride and joy of Florida State University, this 6'3", 235 pounder established himself as one of the most aggressive and feared linebackers in the ACFL while playing for the Roadrunners in 1968. Avery's superior ability held many offenses impotent and at the end of the season his gridiron exploits were recognized and he was signed by the Denver Broncos. Sumner also played for our Richmond Rebels in the season of 1966.

AL WOODALL

There were all smiles in Roadrunner Land as Al Woodall signed a contract joining the professional ranks with our Richmond Roadrunners. Woodall, out of Duke University in 1967, led the Atlantic Coast Conference in total passing yards and highest completion average. A classic drop-back passer, Al led the ACFL in passing in his rookie season with the Roadrunners and was the #2 draft pick of the World Champion New York Jets, where he worked his magic for five seasons.

Football in Richmond

"Sell Those Tickets!"

Central Richmond Association Princesses look on in obvious delight, along with Bill Templeton, Club Owner (left) and Frank Soden of WRNL Radio, as Jim Piersall poses with Miss Linebacker. Jimmy Taylor (lower left) and Gene Huggins also watch with envious grins. The occasion was the season ticket sale kick off cocktail party at the Jefferson Hotel.

Doug McNeill

With the motto of "you play the way you practice," McNeill established himself as an anchor in the offensive line for both our Richmond Mustangs and Roadrunners. As a player-coach for both teams, he led by example and was truly an inspiration to all the "hogs" in the trenches. At 6'1", 200 pounds, Doug was an outstanding lineman at George Washington University, where he gained All-Southern Conference acclaim and Honorable Mention All-American.

AL RAPPOLD

This promising halfback out of Mississippi State University left many a defender quivering with his ball carrying and pass catching abilities. At 6', 195 pounds, Al was an enthusiastic pig-toter for the Roadrunners in 1968. Seen here snaring a pass for a completion, he was known to ramble for additional yards after a reception. Al emerged with the reputation of a winner in the season of 1968.

ROADRUNNERS - "SIS-BOOM-BAHS" 1969

The Roadrunners had a whole covey of pretty cheerleaders for the 1969 season. Pictured here atop of one of Team Owner Bill Templeton's convertibles is the classy squad of revelers. Pictured (l-r) Pamela Templeton, Debbie Jacobs, Carol Boykin, Cheryl Fornash, Brenda Bokkon, Susan Kaufelt, Cindy Wade and Linda Dudley

ROADRUNNERS' NEW LOOK - 1969
Inspecting the Roadrunners' new gold and black helmet are Jim Taylor, famed running back of the Green Bay Packers and the New Orleans Saints; J. D. Roberts, new Head Coach of the Richmond Roadrunners; and Jimmy Piersall, General Manager of the Roanoke Buckskins. Their uniforms are identical to those used by the New Orleans Saints, the Roadrunners' NFL affiliate.

BILL McWATTERS
This 6', 215 pound fullback from Teague, Texas starred for our Rebels, Mustangs, and Roadrunners. A bruising runner, Bill had a glorious collegiate career at North Texas State, where he was voted All-Super Central Texas Fullback. Before coming to Richmond, he had stints in the NFL with the Minnesota Vikings and the Atlanta Falcons. While carrying the ball for our Mustangs in 1967, he averaged over four yards per carry.

1968 Richmond Spiders – Tangerine Victors, 49-42

December 28, 1968 was a red letter day in the annals of Spider football. Our Richmond Spider footballers faced an unbeaten and nationally ranked Ohio University squad, and the Spiders were not given much of a chance to win by the national media. The huge crowd at the Tangerine Bowl was up on its feet time and again, as each team battered the other. The Spiders came out the victor, with one of the greatest offensive exhibitions that football has ever known. Led by Quarterback Buster O'Brien, who ran elusively and passed the ball with the accuracy of a major league pitcher, completing thirty-nine of fifty-eight passes for a school record 447 yards and four touchdowns. This exhibition of aerial fireworks was assisted by the acrobatic catches of All-American Walker Gillette and Richmond's own Jim "Sticky-Fingers" Livesay. There was dancing in the streets of Richmond, Virginia for the Spider rooters, who were delirious with joy.

THIRD QUARTER
The Collegiate Game

First football contest takes place, the year 1881,
University of Richmond challenges Randolph-Macon, the rivalry had just begun
Richmond crosses the goal line, gets one point for each score,
Randolph-Macon ends with zero, need we say anymore.
Many great teams at Virginia Union, to Hovey Field fans went to see
There was even a team downtown, at the school called MCV.
The players oh so great, no room here to name them all
Sanford and Marchant did the blocking, Ralston and Stoudt ran the ball.
When it came to punting, The Spiders can do no wrong,
With names like Bragg and Bruce Allen, kicking the pigskin oh so long.
Lamberti, Chavis and Pat Kelly, all defenders of the rush
When ball carriers would cross their path, their bodies they did crush.
And who could forget the Tangerine Bowl, in the year of '68
Buster O'Brien's passing, did surely seal their fate.
1969 Randolph-Macon team, Coach Keller does put his stamp
The Yellow Jackets from Ashland win playoffs, they're now National Champs.
Then there's Null and Wacker, and oh how Johnny Mack loved the game,
They all played with passion, that's how they gained such fame.
And when the game is over and the final whistle sounds
These college players we'll not forget, the finest in our town!

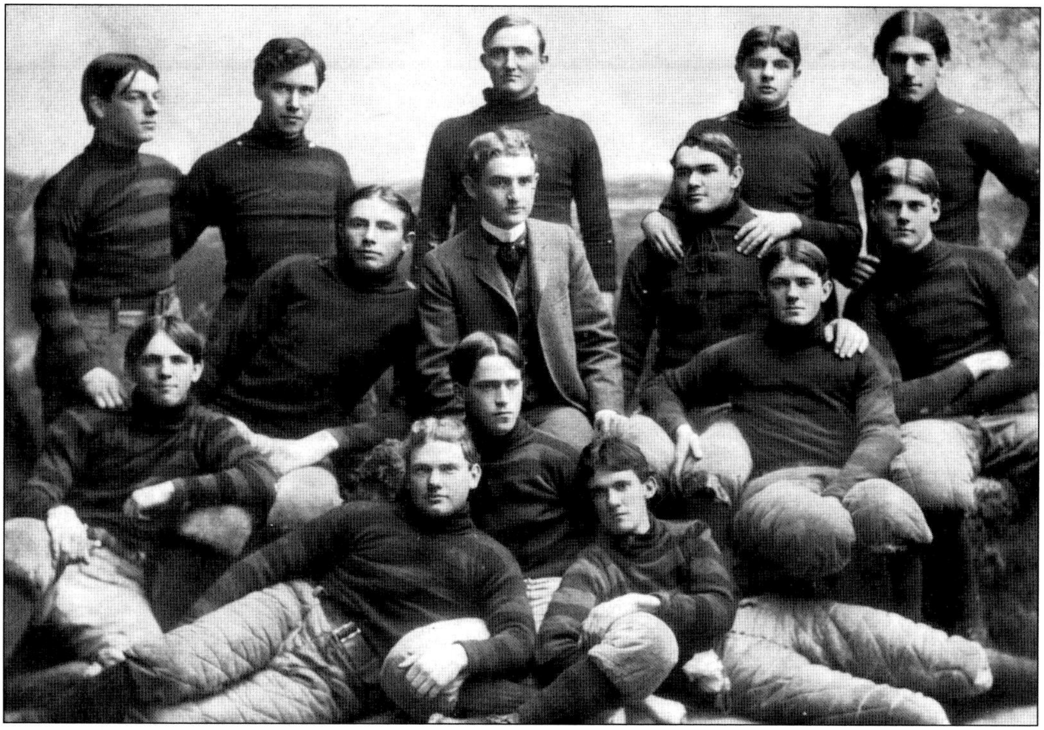

The Collegiate Game

1899 Richmond Spiders

The Richmond footballers did not go undefeated in 1899, but they do, however, pose proudly in this most classic team photo. Coach Hill's heros are dapperly outfitted in the uniforms of the day, consisting of striped jerseys and quilted football pants. Looking passionately at the camera, the players appear to exude poise and confidence, which led this nineteenth century Spider team to a 2-2 season record.

Samuel Stone - 1899 Richmond Spiders Captain

This "Lynchburg Legend" became the star quarterback and captain of the 1899 Richmond gridders. Known to run over and around the opposition, Stone excelled from the quarterback position, leading the Spiders to a .500 season and a 41-0 victory over rival William & Mary.

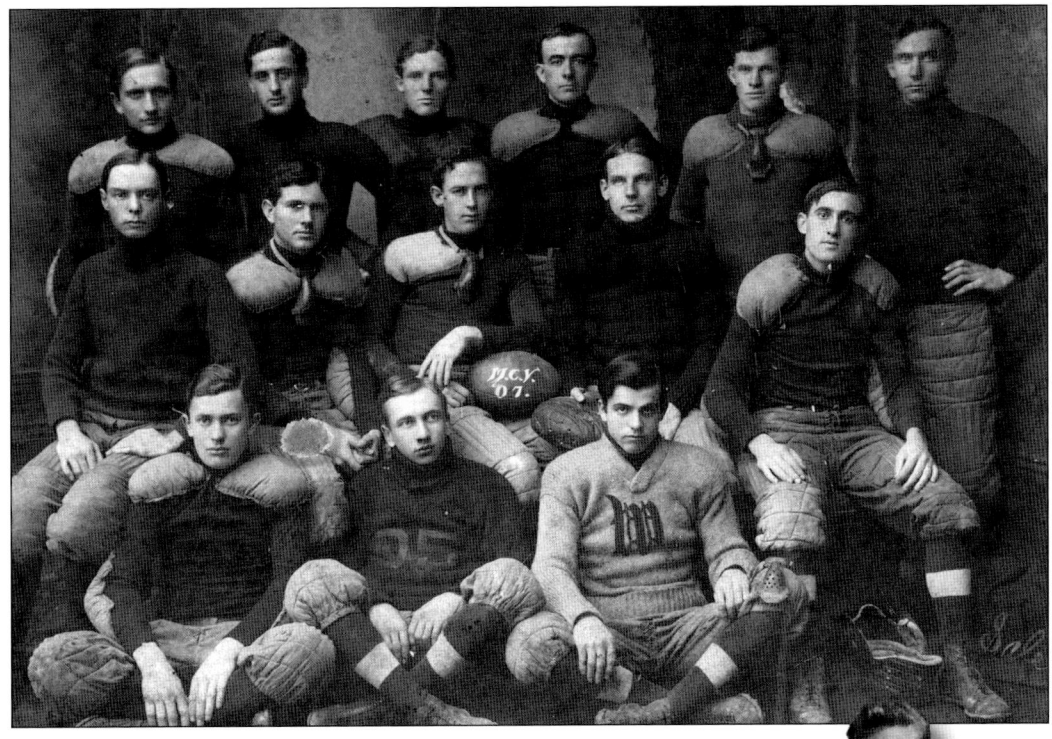

MCV FOOTBALLERS 1907

This photo captures the MCV football team confidently looking the camera square in the eye, with an attitude that they can play with the big boys. This group of quality, tailored footballers, exhibit fine fashion sense in a variety of period uniforms, which include sewn on shoulder pads and nose guards. The team portrait is one of the few items of memorabilia to have survived that chronicles the existence of this team; truly a magnificent relic of Richmond's football earliest days.

EARL STOUDT - RICHMOND SPIDERS 1958-1961

At 5'9" and weighing 173 pounds, Stoudt had no equal at halfback during the 1958-1961 seasons with the Spiders. With his legs lashing out sideways like scythes, Earl would slip off one tackle after another in route to his 22 touchdown career total, while accumulating 3,749 all-purpose yards. Both All-Conference and Honorable Mention All-American in his last two seasons and Southern Conference Player-of-the-Year in 1961, Stoudt has left his footprint on the gridiron at the University of Richmond.

Virginia Union University Gridders

Coach Hucles' football squad of 1938 stares intently as they pose for a team picture in there stylish period football gear. The 1938 footballers featured a freshman running back from Haddenfield, New Jersey by the name of Freddie Cooper. At 5'7" and 175 pounds, he could run like a sprinter through a sliver of an opening or plow like a battleship through a mass of tacklers. The team finished the season amassing an impressive record of 5-2-2, while bringing the huge crowds at Hovey Field up on its feet often with their potent ground attack.

Jesse "Bad News" Chavis - Virginia Union Panthers

There were plenty of bruised bodies when "Bad News" Chavis put the pads to you. This intimidating linebacker demonstrated poise and confidence as a leader of the defense for the Virginia Union Panthers. After a brief stint with the Denver Broncos, Chavis' star showed brightest as the dean of linebackers for our Richmond Roadrunners and Saints. When his playing days were over, Jesse shared his talents as a coach for the Virginia Union Panthers.

Taylor Sanford - Richmond Spiders 1925-1928

This tenacious tackler was one of the best footballers who ever pranced about local gridirons. A four year letterman for the Spiders, Taylor's devastating tackles left pigskin toters staggering around in the backfield. As captain of the 1928 Richmond club, he led with visual emotion and fiery exhortations. Broad shouldered and lean hipped, Sanford repelled many runner attempts to catapult headfirst across the scrimmage line. A shining star for the Spider gridders in the 1920s, Taylor was a two-year All-State selection.

Louis A. Wacker - Richmond Spiders 1952-1955

A chivalrous fighter, Lou displayed superior ability and leadership while garnering All-Conference and All-State awards as a running back and defensive back for the Spiders. In one contest against Wake Forest in 1954, he had three pass interceptions. As his senior year approached, Lou was rated as the top pass defender in the South. After graduation he had a brief career in the NFL with the Detroit Lions. Quite the success as the head coach of the Emory & Henry College football program, Lou led the Wasps to eleven ODAC Conference titles, five trips to the NCAA playoffs, and was named Coach of the Year six times.

Randolph-Macon 1969 National Champions

November 29, 1969, "one of the most storied days in Yellow Jacket football history," as the football team was 47-28 victors in the First Annual Knute Rockne Bowl. The contest pitted the Purple Knights of the University of Bridgeport against our Randolph-Macon squad. An inspired group of Yellow Jacket defenders, led by Doug Moyer and Walt Zyglocke, installed mayhem into the intricate Purple Knights offense, while the offense, led by the blocking of Mike Morris and Tommy Lindsay and running sensation Howard Stevens, rushed to a Macon victory and secured NCAA Division II College Championship to the small town of Ashland, Virginia.

Howard Stevens - Big Game Thriller

Born to run the football, this 5'5", 165 pound back out of Harrisonburg, Virginia, began his legendary college career at Randolph-Macon College in Ashland, Virginia. "When you've got the biggest cannon you shoot it," and that is what Coach Keller did with Howard during the 1968 and 1969 football seasons. Stevens led the 1968 Yellow Jackets to the only unbeaten and untied season in the school's history. In doing so he won the college division rushing championship, gaining 1,468 yards in nine games, an average of 191 yards per game.

MIKE BRAGG - RICHMOND SPIDERS 1965-1967

One of the ultimate "tools of the trade" a coach can have is a consistent punter. The Spiders possessed one in Michael Edward Bragg for the seasons of 1965-1967. Mike had an illustrious tenure punting for Richmond, with a career average of 41.9 yards per punt, while being selected to play in the 1968 College All-Star game. Drafted by the Washington Redskins in 1968, Mike "brought the fans to their feet" with his skyscraper punts and coffin corner kicks. As a 13 year NFL veteran he averaged 39.8 yards per punt, and holds the Redskin's record for most career punts of 896.

EDWARD "SUGAR" RALSTON - RICHMOND SPIDERS 1942, 1946-1948

Hailing from the halls of Thomas Jefferson High School, where he was co-captain and an All-City performer, "Sugar" entered the University of Richmond in 1942. After a three year period serving our military, he performed his magic again for the Spiders in 1946-1948. At 6'1" and 190 pounds, Sugar was afraid of nothing, and eager to do anything the coach asked while plying his trade as both a linebacker and fullback. He ran with the power and speed of a steam engine while smashing and battering would-be tacklers. Co-Captain of the 1948 Spider footballers, "Sugar" was named as the Most Valuable Player in 1946, and was also honored as a Little All-American.

THE COLLEGIATE GAME

BUSTER O'BRIEN - RICHMOND SPIDERS 1966-1968

O'Brien ranks as one of the greatest quarterbacks in Richmond football history. This dean of Spider quarterbacks led the 1968 team to an exhilarating come from behind Tangerine Bowl upset victory over an undefeated Ohio University eleven. In doing so he set records for total offense in one game with 486 yards, most passes completed in one game, 39 completions, and most passing yards in one game, 447 yards. Buster was a two-time All-Southern Conference player and in 1968 was named Southern Conference Player of the Year.

JACK NULL - RICHMOND SPIDERS 1943-1946

Jack Null's exploits on the Richmond gridiron won't soon be forgotten. At 5'9" and weighing 152 pounds, his raw boned body draped in the Spider colors; a small man, but tough, indomitable and spirited. Playing both center and linebacker, Jack was the smallest lineman on the squad, but a demon on defense; he earned All-State credentials in 1945. A bona fide leader on and off the field, Jack captained the Richmond football team in 1946, while later coaching the Spiders' freshman squad for four seasons.

BRUCE ALLEN - RICHMOND SPIDERS 1975-1977

The cheers reverberated throughout old City Stadium as Richmond punter extraordinaire Bruce Allen dazzled the crowd with his booming kicks throughout the seasons of 1975-77. While amassing an impressive career punting average of 40.1 yards, Bruce was at his career best in 1976 with his "crown jewel" of 79 yards against East Carolina. His college credentials led to him being drafted by the NFL's Baltimore Colts. The son of Hall of Fame Head Coach George Allen and brother of former Virginia Governor and Senator George Allen, Bruce presently serves as the General Manager of the Washington Redskins. Excelling as a football front office "magician," he has also served as the General Manager for the Tampa Bay Buccaneers and as a senior executive with the Oakland Raiders.

PAT LAMBERTI - RICHMOND SPIDERS 1955-1957

One of the finest linemen to ever enroll at the University of Richmond, Lamberti made his presence known early. In the trenches he displayed a rough-house, hardnosed brand of football, for which he gained recognition being named to the Virginia Collegiate All-State team on three occasions. After Spider football, Lamberti had a brief career with the St. Louis Cardinals and the Baltimore Colts of the NFL, as well as the Denver Broncos and New York Titans of the AFL. Pat also served as a player-coach for our Richmond Rebels.

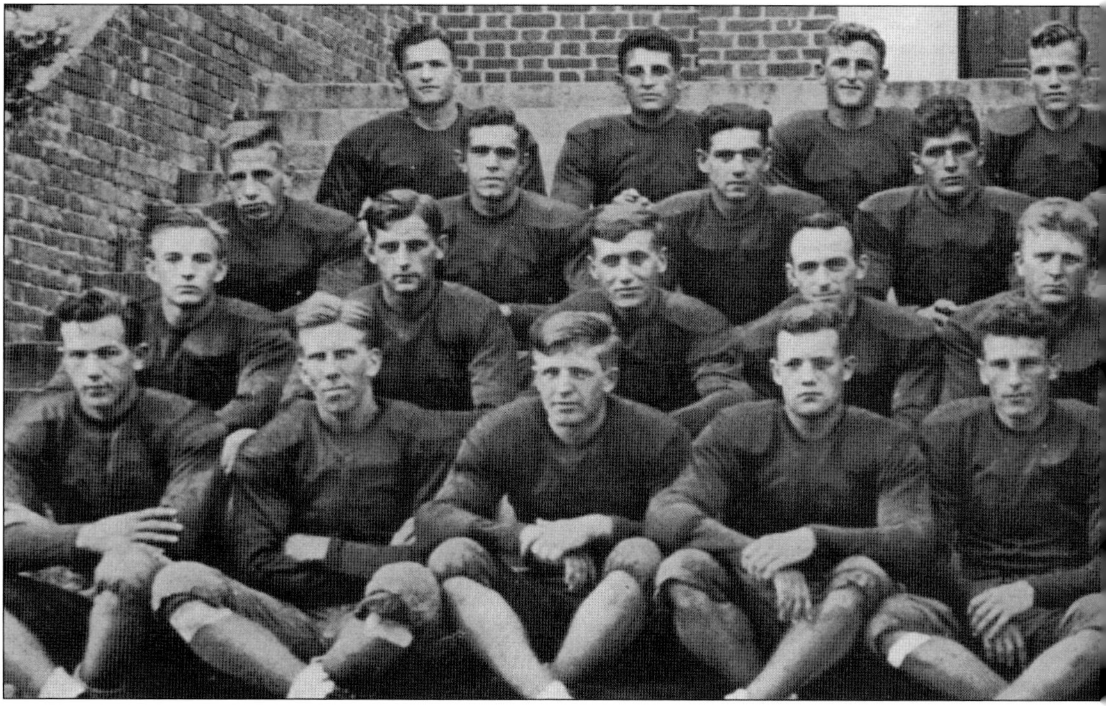

The Collegiate Game

1934 Thistlethwaite's Wonders 8-1

In his first year as Head Coach, Glenn Thistlethwaite guided the Spiders to an 8-1 record, the best winning percentage (.889) of any Richmond football team in the history of the school. Pictured here, Front Row (l-r) Humphries, Leverton, Schulz, Fred Vaughan, Jimmy West,

Union Triumvirate - Anderson, Kelly, Ford

The next step for this triumvirate of beefy Virginia Union lineman was the National Football League. Weighing in at over 770 pounds, they led the Panthers to a 7 win 2 loss record in the season of 1962. Pictured left to right are Roger "Big Red" Anderson, William "Bill" Kelly, and Harlow Fullwood. Kelly signed with the San Diego Chargers, while Fullwood inked with the Baltimore Colts. Anderson, drafted by the New York Giants, had an illustrious four year career with them. A mountain of a man at 6'5" and 265 pounds, Roger provided special excitement to the New York fans with his signature pass rush.

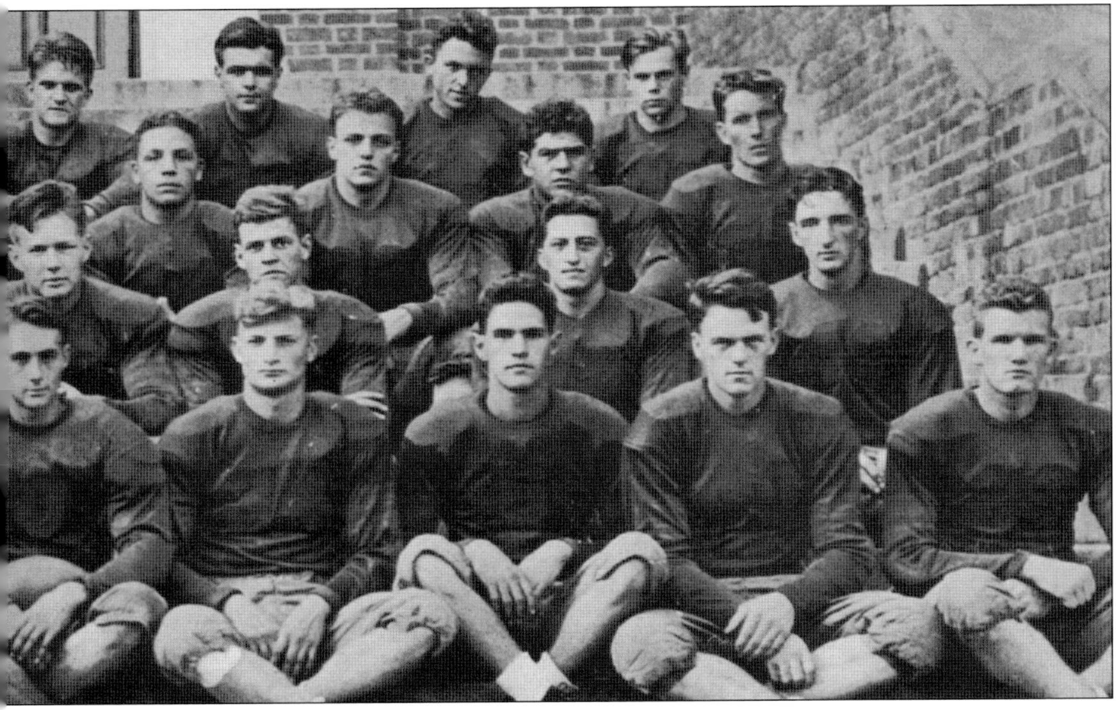

Captain Smithson Morris, Dobson, Garber, R. Todd, Sandford; Second Row (l-r) Brooks, Diedrich, T. Morris, Casey, Walton, Graham, Briggs, Umansky, T. Todd; Third Row (l-r) Schneck, Dickinson, Wrenn, Tenore, Lacy, Botwick, Schaaf, Kassin, Howe; Fourth Row (l-r) Sutton, Pittore, Mike West, Robert Vaughan, Toler, Miller, Robertson, Denton

AVALON B. MARCHANT - RICHMOND SPIDERS CAPTAIN 1938

Known for his leadership and exploits on the Spider gridiron, this "all everything" end had an uncanny skill for attracting the opposition's ball carrier. As captain of the 1938 squad, he led the team to a 6-3-1 record with his intense tackles and spectacular snagging of the pigskin. This photo shows off the form that made him the most feared Richmond footballer of the 1938 season and All-State selection in 1937.

The Collegiate Game

Johnny Mack Brown
Richmond Spiders Captain 1951

At 6' and 195 pounds, this hard hitting center out of Culpepper, Virginia was born to be a leader. Brown excelled in the trenches during his tenure with the Spiders. His textbook form and passion for the game led him to being named Captain of the team in 1951. Equally aggressive on both sides of the ball, John was known for his crisp blocking on offense and his sure tackling on the defensive side of the ball. After his college career he became an outstanding Head Football Coach at Henrico High School.

Erik Christensen, -
Richmond Spiders 1951, 1953-1955

A "stonewall" as a defensive end and an acclaimed gridiron blocker, Eric excelled as a leader of the lineman during his tenure with the Spiders. His precision blocking and tackling propelled him to be the only Virginia collegian selected All-State in football at the same school for four years. Erik had a "cup of coffee" with the Washington Redskins in 1956, after which he jumped to the Canadian Football League, where he starred with the Calgary Stampeders in 1956 and 1957.

GREG GREGORY - RICHMOND SPIDERS

This picture says it all, as Greg shows off the form that made him a most feared quarterback at the University of Richmond during the late seventies. Another "coach on the field," his reputation as a brainy quarterback with a competitive spirit vaulted him to the upper echelons of college coaching. With some thirty years as a college football coach, Greg is well respected for the offensive schemes he implements. His impressive coaching stints include: The University of Virginia, Army, Missouri Southern (Head Coach), University of Richmond, Ohio University, South Florida, and his present position as offensive coordinator at The University of South Alabama. His dedication to the game has made for a most prodigious and intriguing football resume.

RAY EASTERLING - RICHMOND SPIDERS 1969-1971

A dynamic force in the Spiders defensive backfield during his career at Richmond, Ray had a nose for the football, which led to his ten career interceptions, two of which were returned for touchdowns. In his junior and senior seasons he was selected to the All-Southern Conference team and in 1972 played in the Coaches All-American game. In 1972 Ray was drafted by the Atlanta Falcons, where he immediately instilled fear in the opposition receivers who dared cross his path. His eight season career with the Falcons resulted in 13 interceptions, and too many bone crushing tackles to count.

RICHMOND SAINTS PROGRAM 1970

Here is a visually appealing football program for the Richmond Saints of the Atlantic Coast Football League. This "season of turmoil" was highlighted by a decision to go with a youth movement, which featured many inexperienced professional players. Also there were numerous player injuries and the final topping was the exodus of our head coach to the NFL's New Orleans Saints. The Times Dispatch report said it best in their article on the team's final game, "The future of the Richmond franchise following today's game is questionable."

THIRD QUARTER
THE RICHMOND SAINTS

Season of 1970, our Richmond team now called the Saints
Undertake a youth movement, our fine city they'll soon paint
Carrying the ball will be Carlos Bell & Little Ike Brown
Fair and Slade are the pitchers, Szymakowski catching touchdowns
Defenders are in question, of them we don't know
Our linebackers true leaders, namely Chavis and Tom Glasgow
Roberts returns as coach, wondering what this team will do
Start the year with numerous injuries, fan turnout is few
With character and effort, footballers who love to hit
Coach comes out and tells us, these players will "never quit"
Middle of the season, more players came up lame
Indianapolis on the schedule, Commissioner cancels game
Touchdowns are few, victories have not seen
Don't get our first win till October 31st, Halloween
Smell of victory still in air, must maintain this approach
Turmoil shows his face, New Orleans steals our head coach
Pearson a fighter, this tampering he can't stand
Hires Doug McNeill to coach, Dave Robbins second in command
Norfolk comes to town, things still in a stew
Richmond puts up twenty-two points, while winning game number two
Our owner files a suit, New Orleans Saints not our friend
Richmond ends with just two victories, losses there were ten.

J.D. Roberts - Head Coach

Though far from being the largest man on the practice field, Coach Roberts has no trouble in commanding the attention of his players. Head coach of both our 1969 Roadrunners and the 1970 Richmond Saints, Roberts had his work cut out for him as the team turned to a youth movement in 1970. Possessing a tremendous knowledge of the game and a matchless work ethic, he vowed to give Richmond a squad they would be proud of. "We don't promise to win every game, but we do promise to work hard, hit hard, and play good football right up until the clock runs out." Blessed with grit and charisma, this talented ball coach was rewarded for his coaching talent and signed as head coach of the NFL's New Orleans Saints on November 3rd of the 1970 season, replacing legendary NFL great, Tom Fears.

Carlos Bell

Texas sent us a "big" one when Carlos Bell arrived in Richmond. Standing 6'5" and weighing 225 pounds, Carlos truly had a nose for the goal line as he was the Saints "go to" guy in the 1970 campaign. Whether snagging the pigskin from the air or burling over defensive linemen, this fullback out of the University of Houston played the game with passion and a never give up attitude. In Richmond's two victories in 1970, Carlos played an instrumental role, scoring touchdowns in each contest.

AND NEW ORLEANS LOOKS FOR TALENT
With the Richmond club's affiliation with the NFL's New Orleans Saints, the senior team kept an inquiring eye on the development of would be NFL players. Pictured here are (l-r), Bob Whitman, New Orleans Talent Scout; Gene Huggins, Saint Vice President; and Henry Lee Parker, Director of Player Development for the New Orleans Saints, as they watch a Richmond Saints' practice.

IKE BROWN
At 6'1" and 185 pounds, this versatile running back out of Western Kentucky University led the backfield stable for the season of 1970. A gifted runner who carried the ball with faultless ease, Ike was an inspirational leader both on and off the field. Running behind a line that possessed raw and untested skills, he was a "Portrait of Courage" as he bounced back up after many a vicious tackle.

THE RICHMOND SAINTS

LINWOOD HOLTON
GOVERNOR

COMMONWEALTH OF VIRGINIA
GOVERNOR'S OFFICE
RICHMOND 23219

TO THE RICHMOND SAINTS:

    May I offer my best wishes to both the players and staff members of the Richmond Saints for a successful 1970 season.

    I know I speak not only for Richmonders, but for Virginians all over the state, as we look forward to top flight professional football.

Linwood Holton
Governor

GOVERNOR HOLTON IS A SAINTS FAN

This unique letter from the Governor of Virginia, Linwood Holton, is to the Richmond Saints. Governor Holton is offering his best wishes to the players and staff for a successful football season in 1970. He also stated he was looking forward to "top flight professional football." And the rest is history...

RAY DARK

Homegrown, out of Armstrong High School, Ray was known for his quickness afoot and his instinctive pursuit of the pigskin when it was in the air. As a defensive back for our Saints and our Roadrunners he brought many of his Wildcat fans to the stadium to cheer on the hometown favorite. At 5'9" and 175 pounds, Ray was often given the task of matching up with the opponents' finest receivers.

TOM GLASGOW

Taking on the historically significant linebacker (number) 50, Tom excelled for the upstart Richmond Saints in the early season of 1970. Known as a head-splitting tackler, he had a knack for separating the ball from the ball carrier. (None of those one arm ball strips for this linebacker) At 6' and 200 pounds, out of Bridgewater College, he was admired for his aggressiveness and hard hits. As one of the Saints' running backs quipped, "I'm glad he's on our side."

ARCHIE PRATALI - RICHMOND ARROWS

From the ghost of great teams past, this superlative raw boned lineman had no equal as a center for our Richmond Arrow football teams. Known for his explosive blocking and bone chilling tackles, Archie was rated as one of the best players ever to wear an Arrow uniform. Hailing from the halls of ol' John Marshall High School, he played an active and pivotal role in the success of the Richmond Arrows. A member of the first ever Arrow squad (1922), Pratali plied his craft in the trenches for over 14 years, while being named captain in four different seasons. This Richmond gridiron giant (165 pounds) cemented his place in the Richmond Field of Legends with his old school techniques of "hit 'em low and hit 'em hard."

FOURTH QUARTER
RICHMOND FOOTBALL FIELD OF LEGENDS

Richmond has had many, players who gave us pigskin thrills,
At our old City Stadium, as they showcased their football skills.
With names like Chewning and Freddie Cooper, the fans they did roar,
Our Mr. Inside and Mr. Outside, to pay dirt they did soar.
Willard, Barty, and Redden ran the ball, oh so well
Touchdown makers all, and stars in the NFL.
Gillette and Johnny Hilton, leaping through the air,
Defenders all around them, but the pig's bladder they did snare.
In the trenches there was Waddy, Herb Scott and Robert Pratt,
All quite explosive and quicker than a cat.
Playing days are over, coaching they'd pursue,
Merrick, Thalman and Fritz, just to name a few.
Christman, Adams and Ames are true Rebels, Melvin rockets through the air,
Ross and Keller coach national champions, Bunch plays for "The Bear."
Pajaczkowski, Humbert, Kelly and Tate, to Spiders they are true,
Barber and Joyner set Mustang records, opponents they were blue.
Archie Pratali and Harry Seibold, these men gave their all,
To insure we would always have, the game we call foot-ball.
As we view these mighty legends, let's make this point quite clear,
And not forget our favorite, Richmond's own Willie Lanier!

Willie "Contact" Lanier - NFL Hall of Famer

How many fans in the stands of old City Stadium already knew they were witnessing football history, as Willie Lanier and his Maggie Walker Green Dragons squared off against the Armstrong Wildcats. Willie's penchant for making the big play vaulted him to Morgan State University, where he was twice selected to the small college All-American team. Drafted by Kansas City Chiefs of the American Football League in 1967, Lanier quickly established himself as an institution at the middle linebacker position, while enamoring a generation with his aggressive style of play. Willie's fierce bone chilling tackles led to his nickname "Contact," given to him by teammate Jerry Mays. He was named to the AFL All-Star Team in 1968 and 1969, a six time NFL Pro-Bowler, Kansas City Chiefs Hall of Fame, NFL's Walter Payton Man of the Year Award, NFL's All-Time Team, Sporting News' List of the 100 Greatest Football Players, Virginia Sports Hall of Fame, and the Pro Football Hall of Fame. His legendary status established this Richmonder as the greatest Middle Linebacker in NFL history.

Football in Richmond

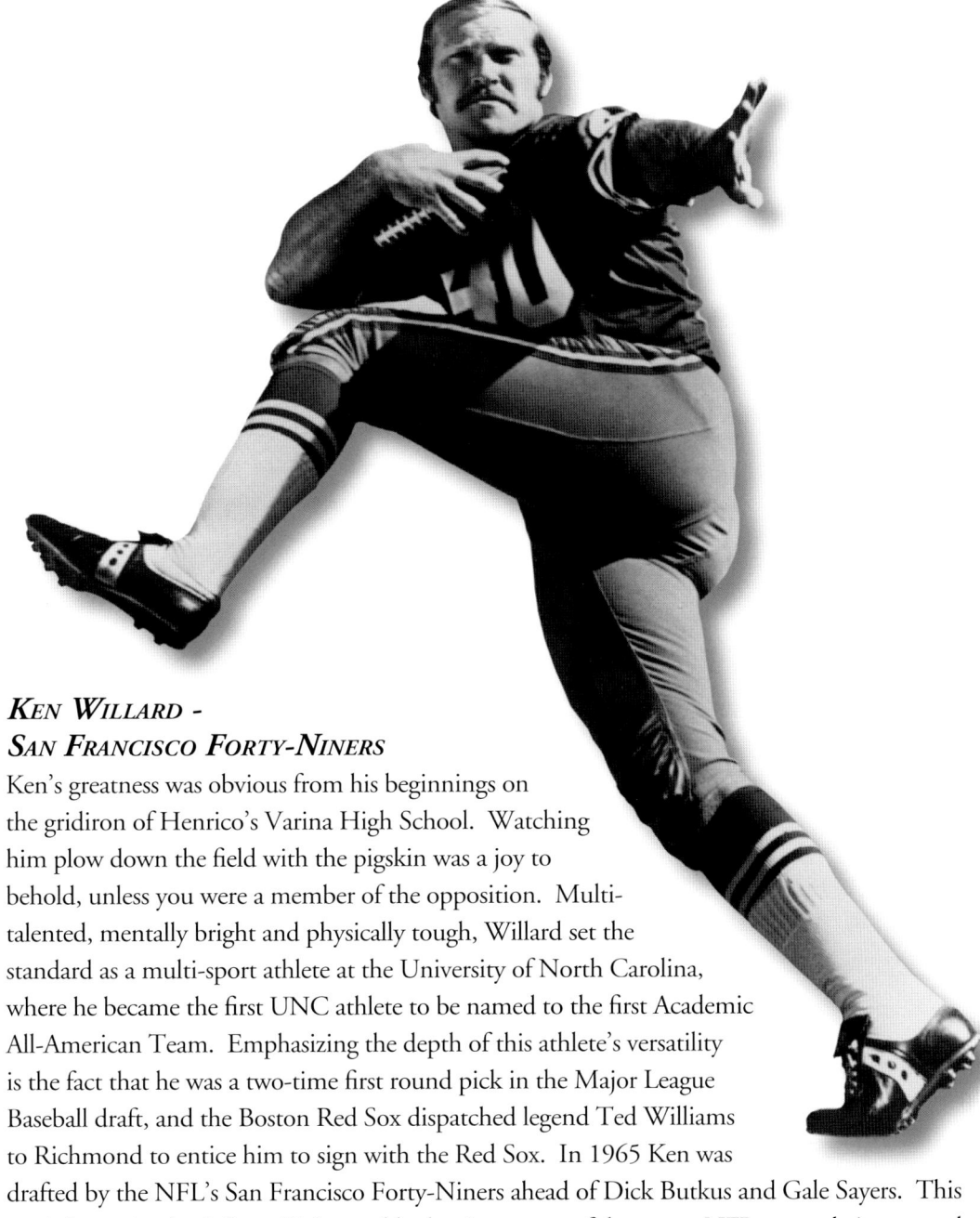

Ken Willard -
San Francisco Forty-Niners

Ken's greatness was obvious from his beginnings on the gridiron of Henrico's Varina High School. Watching him plow down the field with the pigskin was a joy to behold, unless you were a member of the opposition. Multi-talented, mentally bright and physically tough, Willard set the standard as a multi-sport athlete at the University of North Carolina, where he became the first UNC athlete to be named to the first Academic All-American Team. Emphasizing the depth of this athlete's versatility is the fact that he was a two-time first round pick in the Major League Baseball draft, and the Boston Red Sox dispatched legend Ted Williams to Richmond to entice him to sign with the Red Sox. In 1965 Ken was drafted by the NFL's San Francisco Forty-Niners ahead of Dick Butkus and Gale Sayers. This storied running back from Richmond had quite a successful ten year NFL career, being named to the Pro Bowl on four occasions, the Western Division All-Star Team, and induction into the Virginia Sports Hall of Fame. Ken's gridiron aggression while toting the pigskin often made the opposition look like second stringers and his over 6,000 NFL rushing yards immortalizes him in Richmond's Football Field of Legends.

Don "Red" Christman - Boston Patriots

Fearless, imaginative, indestructible, a fighter, are just some of the adjectives that describe the qualities that made this footballer great. Whether starring for the Richmond Spiders or for our Rebels, Roadrunners, and Mustangs, Red left a mammoth imprint on the gridiron at City Stadium. Known for his bone crushing blows, his grit and charisma, he brought the football fanatics to the stadium to view his aggressive play. An All-Star and All-Southern Conference performer, he also won the Jacobs Blocking Trophy. Drafted by the Boston Patriots of the AFL in 1961, Red had a brief career in the pro arena.

Frank M. Dobson - Richmond Spiders Coach

Half-snarling and half yelling, this "old war horse" of a coach delivered his fight talk for the Richmond Spider footballers for some twenty years. Serving the longest tenure on the Spider sidelines, Dobson coached the teams from 1913-1917 and again from 1919-1933. With an overall winning percentage of .503, he demonstrated superior aptitude as an organizer, fundamentalist, and psychologist. As their leader, his mind was packed with action and ideas; his whole being was dedicated to football. He drove home the message he wanted a winner, there were no prima-donnas on Coach Dobson's team.

HERBERT SCOTT - DALLAS COWBOYS

This star guard out of Virginia Union University, where he was on the verge of football immortality, plied his trade for the Panthers from 1971-1975 and was a two-time All-CIAA player and Division II All-American. Drafted by the Dallas Cowboys in 1975, he became a fixture in the offensive line while leading interference for the likes of Tony Dorsett. Dorsett once said, "When Herb goes after a guy, the next thing you see are feet in the air." One of the greatest offensive linemen ever to play for the Cowboys, Scott was a two-time first team All-Pro and three-time Pro-Bowler. At his dazzling best, he helped the Cowboys win Super Bowl XII. Footballer and gentle giant, Herbert truly belongs in the Richmond Football Field of Legends.

JAMES "WADDY" HARVEY - BUFFALO BILLS

The name Waddy Harvey is synonymous with leadership and character. This giant offensive tackle out of Highland Springs High School, played his college ball at Virginia Tech, where he was voted the team's Most Valuable Player in 1968. As a leader of the Hokie defense, he frustrated opposing offenses, thrilling fans and teammates alike with his aggressive style of play. His superlative defensive play while at Tech commanded the attention of the Pros and he was drafted by the Buffalo Bills, where he played for three NFL seasons. He left us much too soon, but the gridiron greatness of Waddy Harvey lends itself to the type of adulation so readily attributable to the heros of our time.

Bobby Ross - Coach Extraordinaire

This thought provoking image depicts the always classy Bobby Ross in his VMI game jersey preparing to unleash the oblong pig's bladder. The photo captures the spirit and grace in which Ross leads his life and instilled in his football teams. A football star at Richmond's Benedictine High School and Virginia Military Institute, Bobby, however, was born to coach. Known as one of the game's most respected coaches, he had the uncanny knack for spotting raw talent and meticulously converting it to a self-confident gridiron warrior. His superlative coaching career included winning the Collegiate National Championship at Georgia Tech in 1990 and guiding the San Diego Chargers to an appearance in Super Bowl XXIX. He has won four different Coach of the Year Awards and the Bear Bryant Award. The name Bobby Ross will forever be chiseled in the Richmond Football Field of Legends.

WALKER "THE BLADE" GILLETTE - CHARGERS, CARDINALS, GIANTS

This man was magical before there was magic! The name Walker Gillette truly defined the term "wide receiver" during his tenure with the Richmond Spiders and the NFL's New York Giants. He had no equal at wide receiver and when he got his hands on the ball, he ran like an antelope. Walker shattered all pass-receiving records at the University of Richmond, catching 158 passes for 2,649 yards and 22 touchdowns. "The Blade" was a consensus football All-American while playing at Richmond, also making four additional All-American teams. Drafted by the San Diego Chargers in

1970, Walker continued driving defenses daffy with his crisp routes and electrifying speed. He played seven years in the NFL, amassing 153 receptions for 2,291 yards and 12 touchdowns.

ROBERT PRATT - COLTS, SEAHAWKS

Robert gained wide attention as a superlative offensive guard while playing for the Saints of St. Christopher's here in Richmond. At 6'3" and 255 pounds, he earned a football scholarship to the University of North Carolina, where he gained All-American honors as a tackle. Drafted by the Baltimore Colts in 1974, Pratt became quite proficient at blocking the roughnecks and misfits of NFL defenses. His incredible focus and determination helped the Colts establish their tradition of winning division titles. Traded to the Seattle Seahawks in 1982, he helped the Seahawks to their very first playoff experience. Known as the "Quarterbacks Best Friend," Robert was named the Seahawks Lineman of the Year in 1983.

Bill Barber - Rebels, Mustangs, Roadrunners

Producing a satisfactory quota of thrills and glowing performances while playing for our Richmond professional football teams during the 1960s, Barber excelled as a star pass snagger. At 6'3" and weighing 210 pounds, he possessed a rare instinct for the football while out wrestling many an opponent for that pigskin. Once he had snagged the ball he could sidestep, shift speeds, pivot and spin, while in pursuit of pay dirt. The battle scarred walls of old City Stadium will never forget his magical moves, as he is enshrined in the Richmond Football Field of Legends.

Chester Fritz - Richmond Rebels

Seen here aggressively pursuing the quarterback, this two time All Big Six and twice second team All-American lineman out of the University of Missouri left a gigantic imprint on the gridirons in Richmond, Virginia. From his playing days with the old Richmond Rebels to his coaching days at Hermitage High School, the name Chester Fritz is synonymous with excellence. An All-League performer for our Rebels, he helped lead them to championship seasons in 1949 and 1950. As the head football coach at Hermitage High School for twenty plus seasons, Fritz set the standard by which all high school coaches before and after would be measured, and guided the Panthers to a state championship in 1958. A juggernaut among men, Fritz's gridiron feats will not be forgotten as he is immortalized in the Richmond Football Field of Legends.

BARTY SMITH - GREEN BAY PACKERS

Barty's chiseled physique stands out among the other Richmond football legends. His legendary career spans his days at Douglas Freeman High School, The University of Richmond, and Lambeau Field as a Green Bay Packer. Would-be tacklers were often left nursing their wounds and pride when encountering his head-on hard hitting style of running. When Barty hung up his cleats, the accolades and achievements were many including High School All-American, All-Southern Conference, two-time Jacobs Blocking Trophy and MVP of the East-West Shrine Game. A first round draft pick by Green Bay in 1974, he had a seven year stay with the Pack, where he won "Offensive Player of the Year" honors in 1977.

FRED "CANNONBALL" COOPER - RICHMOND REBELS

Brimming with emotion, this captivating photo takes you close-up and personal to the man, the player, the coach, the legend that is Fred "Cannonball" Cooper. Seen here at the peak of his popularity as a player with our Richmond Rebels on "Freddie Cooper Day", November 13, 1950, Cannonball pensively accepts gifts and accolades for his outstanding contributions to our Rebels football team. The only unanimous choice for the American Football League's All-League Team, he led the league in scoring and was the league's top ground gainer in 1949. During his tenure as the Rebels premier back, Cannonball turned Richmond's City Stadium into his own private amusement park, with his runs which combined power, speed and a remarkable change of pace. A role model for our youth to emulate, he served as head football coach at Maggie Walker High School from 1960-1971, compiling a 82-18-1 record. As a collegian Freddie was a four time All-CIAA running back starring for the Virginia Union Panthers.

TED KELLER - MACON MASTERMIND

Winning 105 games, this legendary Randolph-Macon College football coach had a knack for putting fire under his teams' tails. A superb teacher and drillmaster, his players displayed flawless execution of the fundamentals of blocking and tackling. During his eighteen year tenure as Head Coach, he won four Mason-Dixon Conference Championships and three Old Dominion Conference Championships. The pinnacle of his victories came in 1969 when the Yellow Jackets won the Knute Rockne Bowl and became the National Small College East Champions. As a player Ted was a brainy Randolph-Macon quarterback with credentials as a co-captain, All-Conference and All-American. With a perpetual twinkle in his eye, Ted led by example and represented the best qualities of Randolph-Macon through his actions on and off the gridiron.

Frank Pajaczkowski - Gifted Spider Runner

Frank could do some totally incredible things with the football as he broke loose for runs from scrimmage of ninety-three and eighty yards during the 1954 and 1955 season. From his fullback position he ran with the power and speed of a locomotive or as one pro scout said, "He's a fullback when he hits the line, but as he breaks through he immediately becomes a halfback, a mighty good one." At 6' and 185 pounds, Pajaczkowski also starred at linebacker for the Spiders, where he was not shy about slugging it out. An All-Southern Conference, an All-State selection; he also starred in the 1956 College All-Star Game against the NFL Champion Cleveland Browns. Drafted by the San Francisco Forty-Niners, Frank had a taste of the NFL. An ambassador for the game and a true gentleman, Frank still resides in Richmond.

John Hilton - Pittsburgh Steelers

At 6'5" and 225 pounds, this tight end out of Hermitage High School and the University of Richmond possessed sticky hands and was considered a big play performer, which led to his nine year career as a NFL tight end. John's intense desire to excel on the gridiron led to his incomparable career as a Richmond Spider, where he was selected to the All-State Team in 1961, 1962 and 1964 and was an All-Southern Conference player in 1964. He was also selected to the Blue-Grey All-Star Classic and the Senior Bowl. During his NFL career, Hilton snagged passes for the Steelers, Packers, Vikings and Lions compiling 144 receptions for over 2000 yards; one of the finest tight ends to ever play the game.

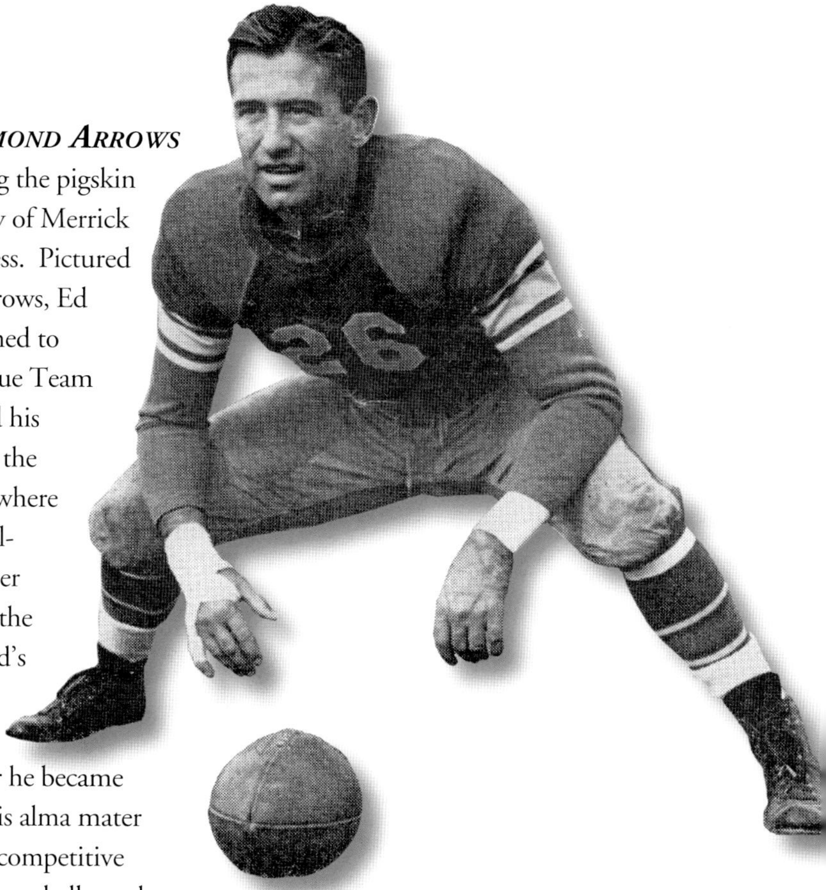

ED MERRICK - RICHMOND ARROWS

This image of Ed snapping the pigskin depicts the power and fury of Merrick in the prime of his greatness. Pictured here as a center for the Arrows, Ed had no equal and was named to the Dixie League All-League Team in 1940. This all followed his exploits on the gridiron at the University of Richmond, where he gained acclaim as an All-Southern Conference center and was elected to play in the College All-Star Game. Ed's fascination with the game did not end when his playing days were over, for he became Head Football Coach at his alma mater in 1944, where he fielded competitive teams for 14 years. A player, a ball coach, a gentleman, and a true Richmond Football Legend.

LELAND MELVIN - TEAM NASA

One of the few athletes who combined smarts, skill and savvy, Leland could have written the book on the science of pass receiving. Ranking as the University of Richmond's new career leader (surpassing Walker Gillette) in pass receptions (198) and reception yardage of 2,669, he was known for his precision routes and YAC (yards after contact). A team captain for the Spiders, he was a leader on and off the field, receiving honorable mention All-American in 1984 and 1985 and Academic All-American in 1985. However, Leland's exploits on the gridiron rank second to his achievement in the real world where he ranks as one of our renowned NASA astronauts.

JIM BUNCH - ALL-AMERICAN

"The quickest, most forceful offensive lineman I have ever coached," stated Paul "Bear" Bryant. This quote by the Bear is all you need to know about Jim Bunch and football. Hailing from the gridiron of Lee-Davis High School, where he was an all everything player, Bunch was destined for greatness. As a freshman at 'Bama he broke into the starting lineup while ripping open holes in the opposition's line big enough for any back to waltz through. A three year All-Southeastern Conference player, Bunch possessed the ideal combination of brains and brawn, while acting as the "Chairman of the Board" for the Tides offensive line. During the season of 1979, Jim spearheaded the charge in leading the Tide to a 12-0 season and Sugar Bowl victory, which vaulted them to National Champions. Jim's flirtation with stardom was rewarded with him being named Associated Press "first string" All-American. And there was dancing in the streets of Tuscaloosa and Mechanicsville...

Bill Joyner -
Rebels, Mustangs, Roadrunners

Never a more liked and admired player, Bill was a mainstay for Richmond's "pro" teams in the 1960s. Not only topping the league as a kicker for our Rebels, Mustangs and Roadrunners, some of his greatest individual performances came as a leader of the offensive line. Joyner's appearance in the huddle seemed to give his running backs a sense of confidence. Totally without grace, totally without form, and the best darn football player around, Bill exemplified everything that is good about football, a true Richmond Football Legend.

Pat Kelly -
Richmond Spiders 1971-1973

There were plenty of bloodied noses possessed by the opposition when this raw boned Richmond linebacker finished a game. In on virtually every running play, Pat was known to bring the crowd to their feet as he pummeled the opponent's running back to the ground with his bone-jarring tackles. His career features include being a three-time All-Southern Conference player, the National Lineman of the Week, and Co-Captain of the Spiders. And was the entire Richmond defense named Kelly's Heroes? In 1974, Pat had a "cup of coffee" with the NFL's Baltimore Colts.

Jake Adams - St. Louis Cardinals

His name is still revered in the halls of old Highland Springs High School and his exploits on the gridiron won't soon be forgotten. This simply amazing image shows the power and fury of Jake in the prime of his greatness. At 6'5", 240 pounds he was a visually imposing figure on both sides of the ball, with uncanny skills as both a blocker and pass receiver. After a phenomenal collegiate career with the Virginia Tech Hokies, Jake caught the eye of the NFL and was drafted by the St. Louis Cardinals in 1964. He also left his mark as a gridiron giant with our own Rebels and Mustangs. An apostle of clean living and fair play, Jake has cemented his place in the Richmond Football Field of Legends. And did you really buy a red convertible with your NFL signing bonus?

Henry Hucles - Virginia Union University Coach

This feisty ol' ball coach, Henry Hucles was a name that truly defined the team in the early years of Virginia Union University football. Whether showing them personally how to block or taking them under his wing as a warm and inspiring father figure, this gifted field general commanded the attention of all who played for him. His dedication and enthusiasm for Panther football was contagious as this legendary football coach compiled 99 victories and a winning percentage of .656 in his 19 year tenure as head coach.

BOB THALMAN - PLAYER-COACH-HUMANITARIAN

From the gridiron of the University of Richmond, to the elevens' of the Richmond Rebels, to the coaching sidelines of Benedictine High School, Bob has left his mark in the annals of Richmond football. A smashmouth guard for the Spiders and Rebels, this former Marine made his greatest contributions as a coach on the sidelines. While coaching at Benedictine, Hampden-Sydney or VMI, all of Thalman's teams possessed a spirit that made them hard to beat. At Hampden-Sydney he won two Mason-Dixon Championships, and holds the longest tenure of any football coach at VMI, where he roamed the sideline for 14 years, winning two Southern Conference Championships. An aggressive leader with a never-say-die spirit, Bob was also known for his humanitarian contributions to society in the founding of "Operation Manhood."

RAY TATE - RICHMOND SPIDERS
"SPAH-DAS WIN, SPAH-DAS WIN"

As a grunt in the trenches, Ray's devotion to his craft was immeasurable. He made an inauspicious debut with the Richmond Spiders in the early 1960s, but by season of 1965 he had All-State and All-Southern Conference credentials and was elected co-captain of the team. As an offensive lineman, precision blocking was his moniker, a testament to his work ethic. Ray possessed a fierce competitive spirit, which he brought to the heat of battle in each and every contest. Upon graduation he served the University as an assistant football coach under Frank Jones for some eight seasons. Ray was seduced into another affair with football, serving as color commentator for the Spider's football radio broadcast. Well known throughout the football community, the name Ray Tate is synonymous with Richmond football.

HARRY SEIBOLD - MAVERICK

A measure of tribute must be afforded Harry Seibold, the owner of the Richmond Rebels in the late 1940s to early 1950s. His uncanny skill at corralling quality coaches and talented gridders was renowned. A testament to this fact was his attracting the likes of Coach Keith Molesworth and the signing of the South's first black professional footballer, Freddie Cooper. Somewhat of a maverick owner, Seibold was able to secure working agreements with both the Chicago Bears and the Pittsburgh Steelers. His work ethic and enthusiasm for the game was contagious. The championship Rebels of 1949 and 1950 commanded national attention, with thoughts of Richmond joining the All American Football Conference. This Richmond football legend was the architect and mastermind behind the Rebels success.

Barry Redden - Rams, Chargers, Browns

With the reputation as a workhorse, Barry toted the pigskin a school record for a season 335 times during his senior year at the University of Richmond. In 1981 he ranked third in the nation in rushing with over 1600 yards and was surpassed only by Herschel Walker and Marcus Allen. His feats of dexterity were well recognized by the pros and he was drafted in the first round of the 1982 draft by the Los Angeles Rams. A fearless running back, Barry played with character and intelligence at the highest skill levels during his nine NFL seasons.

Dick Humbert - Philadelphia Eagles

This 6'1", 180 pound end from Suffolk, Virginia displayed his prowess on the gridiron of City Stadium for the University of Richmond Spiders from 1938-1941 and for the NFL's Philadelphia Eagles 1941-1949. Truly a stellar performer for the Spiders, he brought many a fan to their feet with his amazing leaping catches of the pigskin while proclaiming All-State status. His career with the Eagles was highlighted by his being named NFL Rookie of the Year and All-Pro in 1941. His passion for the game led him back to the University of Richmond, where he plied his trade as a coach for ten seasons.

DAVID AMES - NEW YORK TITANS, DENVER BRONCOS

A versatile football star who combined extraordinary athleticism with quick thinking, David's gridiron abilities spoke volumes. Whether lugging the pigskin to pay dirt, defending the pass, returning punts, or perfecting the science of punting, his presence captured the essence of the event. As a Spider, David was a two-time All-Southern Conference performer, as well as voted to the All-State Team in 1959. In 1961 he played with both the New York Titans and the Denver Broncos of the American Football League, where he put up impressive numbers both on offense and defense. Ames ended his football career while starring for our Richmond Rebels and Mustangs. For all his glitzy numbers and individual accomplishments, it was the manner in which he treated his fellow man that makes him a true Richmond Football Legend.

LYNN CHEWNING - RICHMOND REBELS

This poignant photo depicts Lynn's tenacious expression, which indeed signals the starting point for a mad dash to the end zone during his playing days as a Richmond Rebel footballer. This homegrown Richmonder, who was all-everything for the St. Christopher Saints, went on to star at Hampden-Sydney College. He was All-State for two years and was a star halfback for the United States Military Academy. A multi-talented athlete, Lynn excelled on both offense and defense, and was also known for his superior punting ability. His explosive running style contributed greatly to the Richmond Rebels championship seasons of 1949 and 1950.

High School Classics

FOURTH QUARTER
HIGH SCHOOL CLASSICS

There was Maggie Walker v Armstrong, John Marshall v TeeJay,
Known as the classics, these games they would play.
You didn't win this one; there'd be a year of much teasin'
A victory against your rival would make the whole season.
Oh what a spectacle, fashion, cheerleaders and bands,
Year was '68; thirty thousand spectators filled the stands.
All of this hoopla, surrounding this one game,
Many of the opponents knew each other's first names.
Coaches did inspire, to the players they stood tall,
Wildcats had Maxie, Green Dragons ol' Cannonball.
Jayem had Denton, Hollingsworth and Satt Anderson, to name a few,
TeeJay's were Carmack and Cooper, the players looked up to.
And oh what a game, December 7, 1946,
Glen Allen v Highland Springs, the Tobacco Bowl mix
Burrell led his Springers; Gasser's Panthers could fly,
Springers 6, Panthers 6, game ended in a tie.
1959 matched up again and playing for gold,
Hermitage 13, Highland Springs 2 known as the Hurricane Bowl.
If your photo's not here, we hope you're not sad,
Some we couldn't find, some were just bad.
But we dedicate this book, to all who played the game,
You're all official members, of the Richmond Football Hall of Fame.

High School Classics

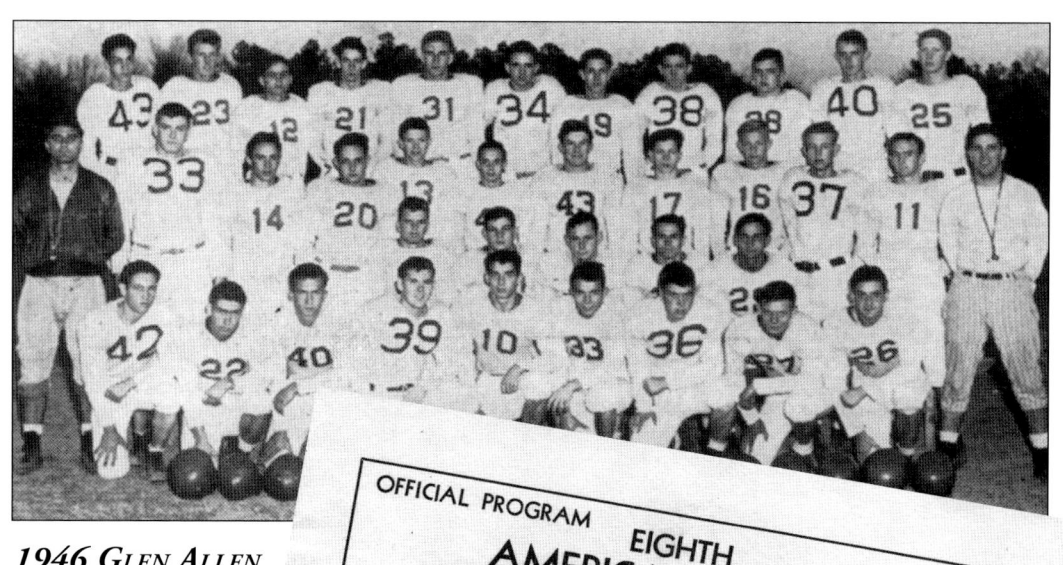

1946 Glen Allen Team

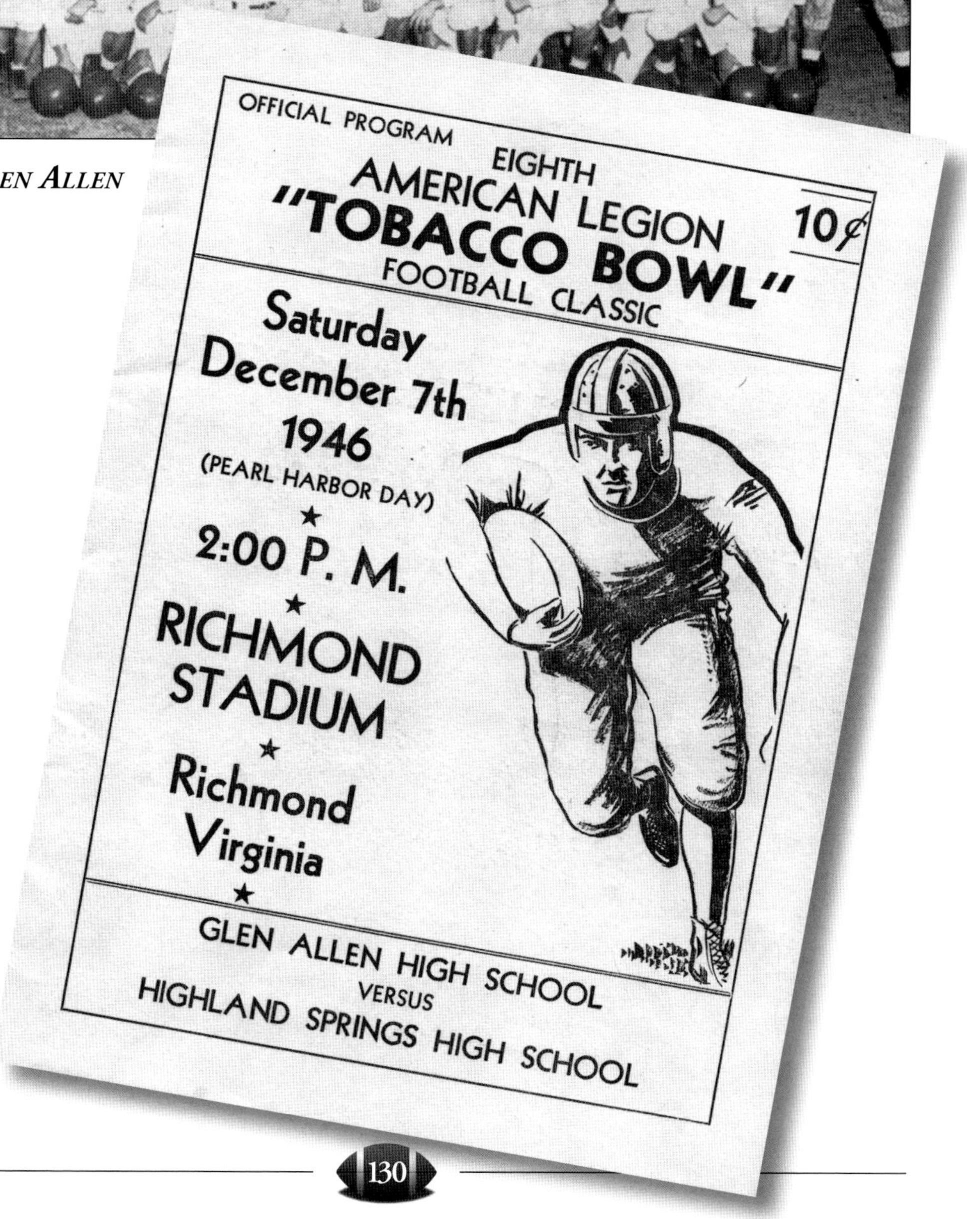

1946 Highland Springs Team

December 7, 1946 Tobacco Bowl Classic
Highland Springs Holds Glen Allen to 6-6 Deadlock.

On this brilliant autumn Saturday afternoon, before a raucous 10,000 footballites, Highland Springs High School's underdog football eleven took on Glen Allen's powerhouse, who had a spotless record for three years and 28 straight victories. The Springers were bringing a 9-0 record into the contest, while amassing 236 points and only giving up 45 points. Glen Allen had scored 319 points and allowed only 13, and also had a 9-0 record. Highland Springs led by their field general, Quarterback Dick Goodman (right) and their all-everything running back Junie Needham, took a first period 6-0 lead on a four yard off tackle run. Glen Allen's Robert Bennett led all runners, picking 181 yards in 31 carries and a touchdown. However, the hero title for this day belonged to Coach Dick Burrell's defensive team, which turned in a stellar performance and held the Panthers' high powered offense to a meager six points. The spectators and players will forever pridefully reserve the fond memories which this spirited football classic provided.

Dick Goodman

High School Classics

1938, Justices Turn Back Thomas Jefferson 19-0

Led by swivel-hipped captain Tommy Moncrief, the Justices of John Marshall defeated their crosstown rivals Thomas Jefferson 19-0 on this rain soaked Saturday afternoon. "A Miserable day for football, but the fourteen thousand fans didn't pay one bit of attention to the chilling wind and stinging rain." Captain Moncrief ripped through the Red and White defense for 122 yards and two touchdowns. The Justices' Paul McMullen had the defensive gem of the day, with a pass interception. Teejays' Speedy Billy Whitehead dashed around the Justices' flanks for 85 yards, as the leading ground gainer for the Jeffs.

November 27, 1948: Wildcats Snuff Out Green Dragons 7-6

On this warm sunny Saturday afternoon, over twenty thousand hooting and howling fans packed into Richmond's City Stadium to watch the Eleventh Annual Armstrong-Maggie Walker Classic. The game was highlighted by the teams' stingy defenses who performed with a swagger, accounting for eighteen total punts in the contest. The Green Dragons were the first to reach pay dirt in quarter one when Quarterback Charles Williams maneuvered through the Wildcats line for a score. From that point until the fourth quarter the game evolved in a course of "Punting 101." In the fourth quarter, the Wildcats were being shutout, Coach Maxie Robinson employed a little trickery with Sam Thompson scoring on a "double reverse" and William Powell bulled through the Walker line for the extra point and Wildcat victory.

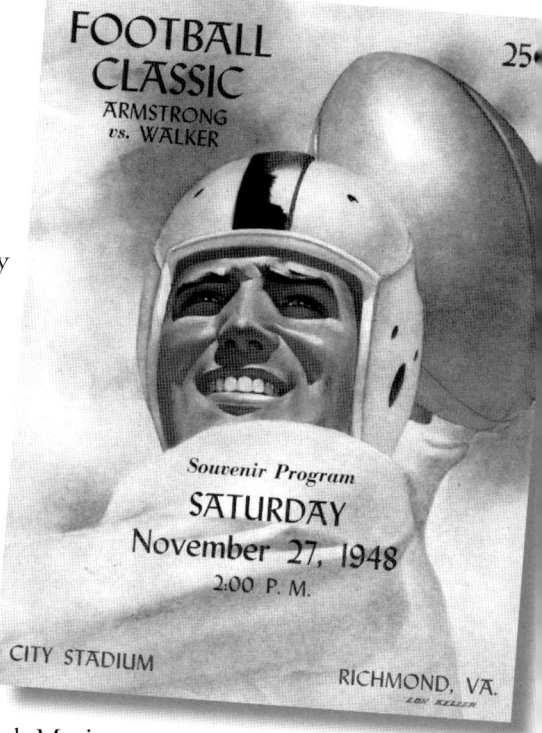

Football in Richmond

John Marshall - McGuire's Battle to Scoreless Tie

"Foes fail to reach decision in bitter game at Tate Field", spoken by sports writer Dave Herman of the Richmond Times-Dispatch. It was a thrilling, soul stirring, rip-snorting tussle for honors, with the ball swinging up and down the field like the pendulum of a clock. John Marshall's unbeaten football team was within two feet of victory in the city's title game with McGuire's, before 3,500 smitten fans at historic Tate Field. In the third quarter, with victory trembling in the balance, the "Byrd Parkers" defense "braced at the supreme moment and held like Gibraltar, as Clarence Oliver, fullback of the Marshallites was stopped at the two foot line, on his attempt to hurdle over for a touchdown." The "preppers" of McGuire's were well led by their Captain Ray Brinser and Bill "Old Grizzly" Thomas, who had already chalked up twelve touchdowns for the season. Leading the Justices was Captain Peaco Todd, who was an absolute dynamo on the gridiron, whether making tackles or toting the pigskin. This scoreless tie for the City of Richmond's prep school championship came as a tribute to the faithful, determined, and hard work of the two prep elevens; equal in strength, equal in ability, equal in skill, and they proved they were as great as one another.

High School Classics

NOVEMBER 29, 1952: ARMSTRONG ANNIHILATES MAGGIE WALKER 27-7

The Armstong team, which Head Coach Maxie Robinson proclaimed was his "best ever," took no prisoners on this cold wintery Saturday afternoon. Coach Robinson unleashed a stable of hard hitting and high stepping running backs who assembled in the Green Dragon end zone

on four separate occasions. The Wildcats amassed 316 total yards, and were led by touchdown heroes John Quarles, Howard Reynolds, Bill Whaley and Charles Porter. Armstrong's run defense put on a clinic, allowing the Green Dragons a mere forty yards on the ground. This fifteenth classic was witnessed by over 14,000 exuberant football fans.

1952 Armstrong Team

1952 Maggie Walker Team

1942: JUSTICES TROUNCE TEEJAY 25-7

"Halted momentarily by TeeJay's deception and trickery, John Marshall loosened all its football might to demoralize, then crush, a plucky TeeJay eleven." Thomas Jefferson's Coach Shelburn Carmack had promised "something new," which was a "spread" formation, seldom seen in high school ball. "The Jeffs ran so often from a spread formation, the Justices wondered where the bread was for their victory sandwich." This was a glorious victory for the Justices, but the day was Quarterback Ray Marshall's, who picked off a Jeff pass from out of the air late in the opening period behind his own goal line and hoofed it 102 yards to pay dirt. Eighteen thousand "hooting and hollering" fans viewed Marshall's magical afternoon in which this Jayem Co-Captain amassed 138 yards on the ground and two touchdowns. When he wasn't toting the pigskin, his fellow Co-Captain Jack Ittner was gaining 122 yards and scoring a touchdown. Providing the holes for this duo was an outstanding line led by Bill Farmer, George Smith, Clyde Metzger, Jack Hoffman, Yippy Collier, George Cooper and Raymond Cash. And let's not forget Governor and Mrs. Darden presence and the fabulous "Sally Rand" reverse, whereby Clyde McAllister waltzed untouched into the end zone!

Football in Richmond

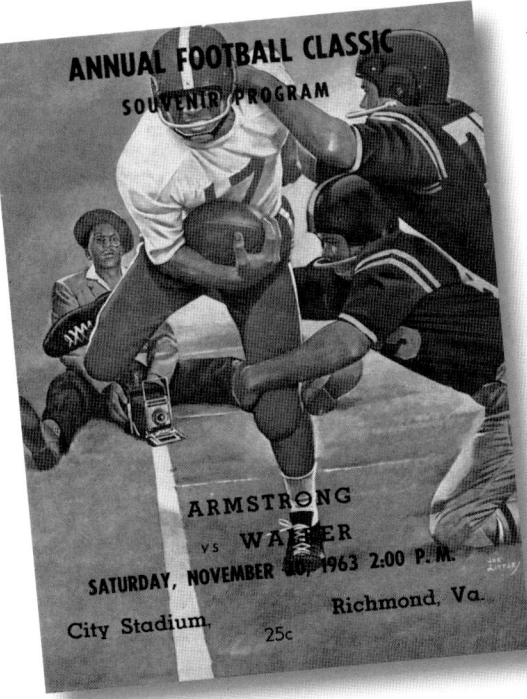

November 30, 1963: Dragons Defeat Wildcats 27-7

With the wounds still raw from President John F. Kennedy's assassination some eight days earlier, over 18,000 spectators with pennants and blankets showed up to cheer their team to victory in this twenty-sixth Walker-Armstrong Classic. On this cool, crisp autumn afternoon, the Maggie Walker defense performed superlatively, only allowing the Wildcats to score seven points. The Green Dragon's most glorious figure of the day was speedy halfback Daryl Johnson, who sprinted through the Wildcats defense for a thirty-two yard touchdown scamper on Walker's first play from scrimmage. Later in the fourth period, "Touchdown" Daryl snatched the pigskin from a defender and proceeded to pay dirt to seal the Maggie Walker victory.

November 19, 1926: Marshallites Mash Cadets 20-0

Before a howling mob of 2,500 electrified fans at Tate Field, the Justices of John Marshall wrecked the dream of the fighting Cadets of Benedictine. As one exuberant fan stated, "these Cadets are fighters, they are game to the core." However, the day belonged to the Justices, who were led by their star running back Peaco Todd and Captain Joe Bentley. Todd zigzagged 65 yards for Jayem's first touchdown on a punt return. He proved to be a veritable thorn in the side of the Cadet gridders by also "flipping passes and catching a few himself." Captain Joe Bentley showed his best form of the season by snatching Quarterback Magill's passes from the air and toting the pigskin to pay dirt. The Cadet eleven were led by Captain Joe Lucas and center Little Willie Ahern.

NOVEMBER 25, 1960: JEFFS ROUT JUSTICES 48-6 IN 30TH ANNUAL TILT

The Jeffs of Thomas Jefferson rolled up 306 rushing yards and the highest number of points (48) by either team in the 30 game series. TeeJay was led by their breakaway halfback, Bobby Magill, who electrified the spectators with his magical moves while gaining 144 yards rushing, scoring three touchdowns, kicking five PATS, and intercepting one pass. This was quite an

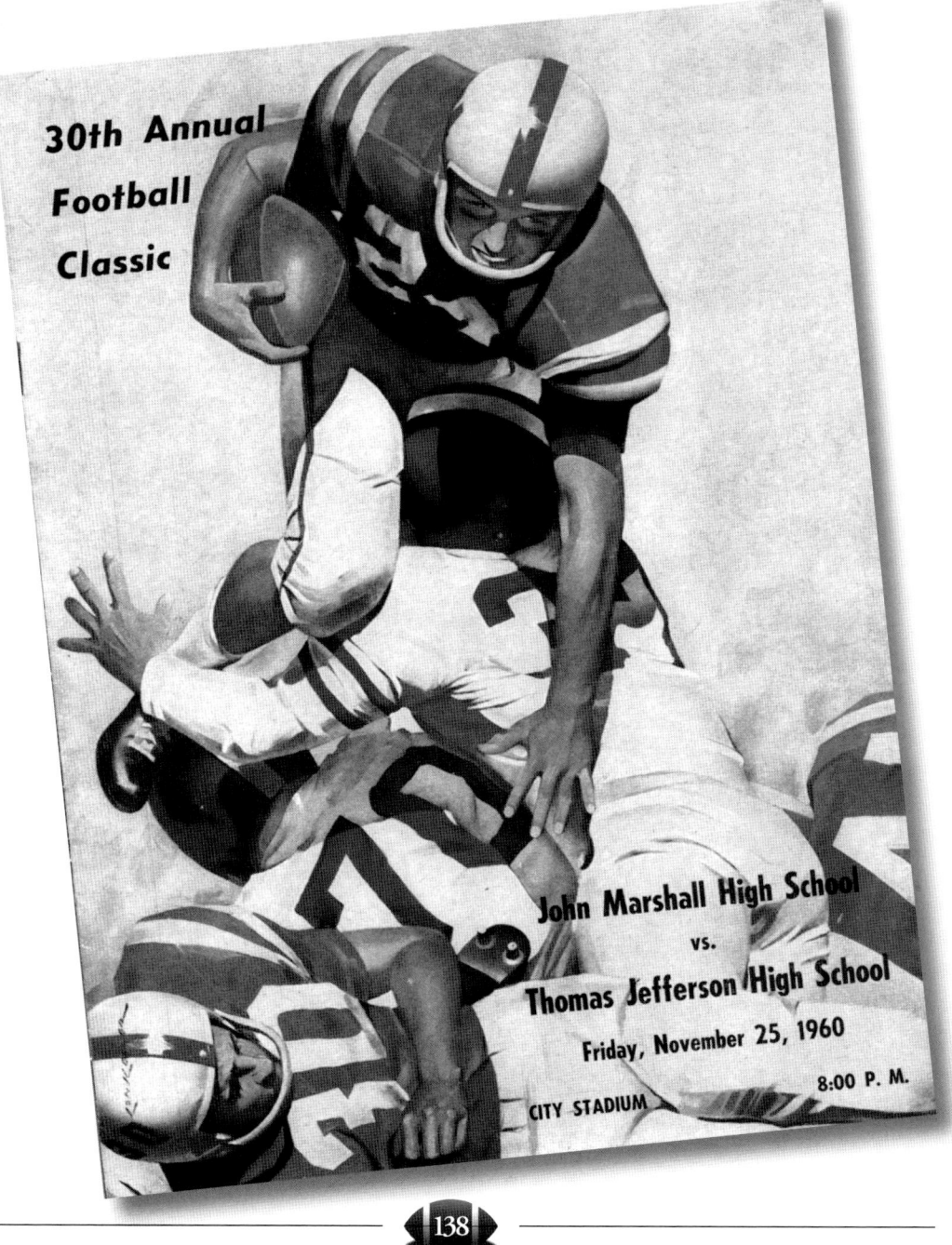

impressive offensive performance by Mr. Magill and the Jeffs. The defense was led by hard hitters Ed Garthright and Bobby Waters. The only ray of sunshine for the Justices was the tosses of rifle arm quarterback C. G. Winston, who threw for 166 yards and one touchdown on a "circus" catch by future North Carolina State star Lloyd Spangler.

1960 THOMAS JEFFERSON TEAM

1960 JOHN MARSHALL TEAM

High School Classics

Tomato Bowl 1963: Byrd Hall's touchdown sweep seals Confederate victory over Patriots, 12-0

1950: Jerry Pugh's touchdown gallops lead Benedictine to 53-0 shellacking of St. Christopher's.

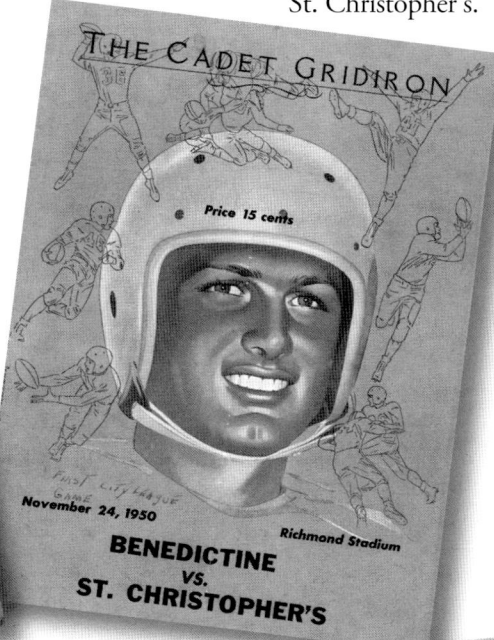

1944: Led by Captain Tom Stanley and the entire defensive unit, the Jeffs jolt the Justices 7-0

1944: Raymond Ross and the Green Dragons whack the Wildcats 20-0!

FOOTBALL IN RICHMOND

1924 Saint Christopher's football eleven, led by center captain Brown and left end Kemper, finished the season with a 3-2-1 record.

Thomas Jefferson and John Marshall footballers line-up for opening kickoff in this 1952 classic, and the victor was?

THE WAY WE WERE

OVERTIME
THE WAY WE WERE

THE HOTCHKISS FIELD SWEEP!!
Do you recognize any of these future gridiron greats? If so, give us a call.

MY FOOTBALL HERO
Can you identify this future high school football star and this Richmond Rebel star?

OVERTIME
ABOUT THE AUTHOR

With the zealousness of a child, Ron Pomfrey (with his football idol Johnny Unitas) has been a researcher of sports history in Richmond and an avid collector of sports memorabilia for the past 35 years. It is with this enthusiasm he has compiled the treasures and knowledge and pure love for the game to write this book. He is forever searching for additional memorabilia and always happy to share his knowledge and expertise with fans and collectors. Ron's future books that are in the planning stages include The Richmond Braves and Richmond Sports Memorabilia.

As a lifelong resident of Hanover County, Ron both taught and coached for 10 years in Hanover County Schools. For the past 21 years, he has been a broker for Ron Pomfrey Realty, Inc.

Football In Richmond

THE END... ZONE

Many Happy Touchdowns!